For Fred and Batoho

Roy Hammonia

Seattle '06

Minidoka Revisited
The Paintings of Roger Shimomura

William W Lew

with contributions by

Roger Daniels
Krystal Reiko Hauseur
Eric L. Muller
Daniel Wueste
Susan L. Smith

Lee Gallery
Clemson University

Distributed by
The University of Washington Press
Seattle and London

This catalog was printed on the occasion of the exhibition
Minidoka Revisited: The Paintings of Roger Shimomura at the
Lee Gallery, Clemson University, September 12, 2005 — October 21, 2005

Cover image   Roger Shimomura, *Minidoka #3 (Diary)*, 1978

Photo Credits   Roger Shimomura

Published by   Lee Gallery
Clemson University
Clemson, South Carolina 29634

Designer   Jessica Barness
Printer   The R.L. Bryan Company, Columbia, South Carolina
Distributor   University of Washington Press, P.O. Box 50096,
Seattle, Washington 98145-5096

Library of Congress Cataloging-in-Publication Data
Lew, William W
Minidoka Revisited: The Paintings of Roger Shimomura
William W Lew; with essays by Roger Daniels, Krystal Reiko
Hauseur, Eric L. Muller, Susan L. Smith, and Daniel Wueste

ISBN 0-295-98583-6

The printing of this catalog is supported in part by a grant
from Furthermore: a program of the J.M. Kaplan Fund.

Additional funds for the printing of this catalog were received
from the following units of Clemson University:
Clemson University Vending Committee
College of Architecture, Arts and Humanities (McClure Endowment)
Department of Art
Lee Gallery
Presidential Colloquium Program
Robert J. Rutland Center for Ethics

Contents

Foreword

Denise Woodward-Detrich

On some level, everyone has experienced the painful realities of being different. Words and deeds issued forth by some may prove to be oppressive and degrading to others, setting them apart from the larger populace. *Minidoka Revisited: The Paintings of Roger Shimomura* explores issues of differences as seen through the life experiences of both Shimomura and his grandmother, and through those of the Asian American community at large. Indeed, *Minidoka Revisited* is intended as an examination of ethnic/racial stereotyping.

The paintings in this exhibition were selected from several important series of works created by Shimomura over a twenty-five year period of time. Selections from the earlier series, including his *Minidoka*, *Diary*, and *American Diary* series, chronicle his family's experiences leading up to and during their incarceration at the Minidoka Relocation Center in south-central Idaho. Selections from the more recent series, including his *Stereotypes and Admonitions* series, reveal "snapshots and stories" of actual experiences of racial/ethnic insensitivity and discrimination that the artist and other Asian Americans have faced in recent history.

Shimomura's work operates on two levels. The paintings invite the viewing audience in with visually stimulating canvases filled with color, comic strip detailing and familiar icons. Upon closer inspection, however, the viewing audience is confronted with the stark reality of human actions. The artist lures his viewers in just long enough to disarm them and then deftly drives home the omnipresent plight called discrimination. Shimomura's approach to visual communication sparks a response and provides a springboard for dialogue and conversation.

Together, these paintings reveal an element of contemporary America that can be mean in spirit and lacking in tolerance to those who appear different. Vivid and pointed, the works reflect one Japanese American's response to an insensitive and sometimes hostile American culture. This exhibition invites its viewing audience to consider how issues of stereotyping and discrimination have impacted a post 9/11 world and to offer a reflective view of America's actions sixty years ago under similar circumstances.

Minidoka Revisited prompts its viewing audience to question past actions, to consider current political environments, and to explore the safety of their own individuality within contemporary America. For these reasons, I felt compelled to bring *Mindoka Revisited* to the Clemson University campus. The paintings of Roger Shimomura are important for our time, and I am delighted for the opportunity to exhibit this body of works in Lee Gallery.

As Clemson University moves forward in its pursuit of excellence, it is fitting that an exhibition of this kind be a part of the university experience for students, faculty and staff alike. Most importantly for Clemson, the exhibition poses poignant questions to all viewers regardless of gender, generational, cultural, or ethnic/racial differences. Who we are, how we act, and what we contribute to society are questions that students explore daily in their education. Shimomura's work prompts us to ask the following: Could this be a situation I have to contend with on a daily basis? How would I respond to similar situations? Could this happen to me today under a different set of circumstances? Have I participated in this kind of stereotyping without realizing my own actions?

I suspect that we would do well to reflect on the issues prompted by the paintings of Roger Shimomura. From my perspective, much can be gained from a close scrutiny of the works of this important artist.

I am greatly appreciative of the team of dedicated individuals who diligently worked towards the realization of this project, and of the many others who supported their efforts. Three years in the making, this project proved to be one of Lee Gallery's most complex under-takings in recent years. The collaborative nature of this project, the quality of research poured into it, the willingness of everyone involved to work collectively towards a common goal, and the significance of the work and artist, make this project a perfect model for future programming in Lee Gallery.

I would like to thank the collectors for their generosity and their willingness to share their works with us for this exhibition. Without their support there would not be a *Minidoka Revisited*. A special thanks is due the Greg Kucera Gallery in Seattle. Mr. Kucera and his staff not only loaned us works from the gallery but coordinated matters related to the shipping of the art works from collections on the West Coast, Idaho, and Chicago to Clemson University.

I would also like to thank Roger Daniels, Krystal Reiko Hauseur, William W Lew, Eric L. Muller, Susan L. Smith and Dan Wueste for their time, and insightful essays in support of this project. Their perspectives highlighted the intent of this exhibition and enriched our under-standing of the works in it.

The programs of the Lee Gallery would not exist were it not for the dedicated efforts of its supporters and volunteers. I would like especially to acknowledge the law firm of Wyche, Burgess, Freeman & Parham of Greenville, South Carolina, for a significant contribution that made possible several of the programs planned in conjunction with *Minidoka Revisited*. My gratitude and thanks to our gallery volunteers who addressed many of the details related to this project and to the day-to-day operations of Lee Gallery. I would also like to thank the Friends of Lee Gallery, and, especially, Patti McAbee, our Board President, for their tireless determination to raise awareness and appreciation of the visual arts on campus and for their enthusiastic support of *Minidoka Revisited*.

Lastly and especially, I would like to thank President James F. Barker and First Lady Marcia Barker for their continued support of Lee Gallery and for their vision of a "Top 20" Clemson University that integrates visual arts experiences for all of our students. Their combined leadership, enthusiasm, encouragement, and support make the visual arts an important component of the Clemson Experience.

Denise Woodward-Detrich
Director, Lee Gallery
Clemson University

Preface and Acknowledgments

William W Lew

Minidoka, located in the desert region of south-central Idaho, references one of the most tragic and unfortunate episodes in American history. It and nine other sites, all located in remote and desolate regions of the United States, served as home to approximately 120,000 persons of Japanese ancestry (70 percent of whom were American citizens) in the aftermath of the bombing of Pearl Harbor. The title of this project was inspired by the name of the relocation center in south central Idaho where approximately 10,000 persons of Japanese ancestry from the Pacific Northwest (including the artist and his family) were incarcerated during the tumultuous years of World War II. The title also references several series of paintings by Shimomura that were greatly influenced by what we might call the Minidoka or "camp" experience.

Given the comparisons that have been made in the past several years between December 7, 1941, and September 11, 2001, it only seems appropriate that on the eve of the 60th anniversary of the closing of Minidoka and the other nine detention centers, we make an effort to "revisit" and reflect on some of the issues related to those tragic events. These paintings by Roger Shimomura provide us with an appropriate and insightful vehicle for doing so. This exhibition includes works by this Japanese American artist that span some two and half decades. The content of these works deals not only with issues related to the Minidoka experience but also to similar issues that have caught the attention of many in a post 9/11 world. The common threads that relate one to the other include racial/ethnic stereotyping and what I refer to as "misidentification" within the context of stereotyping. Because the issues broached extend well beyond the formal considerations of the visual arts, the individuals invited to prepare essays for this catalog were drawn not only from art disciplines, but also from other academic disciplines as well. Further, these individuals were encouraged to look at the issues touched upon in the paintings from within the context of their academic disciplines.

A project of this kind could not have been realized without the help, encouragement, and resources of many. I am first and foremost indebted to Clemson University for a sabbatical leave and to our College of Architecture, Arts and Humanities for a grant that allowed me the opportunity to conduct the preliminary research for this project. I am also grateful for the support that I have received from various units within the University, specifically for the development and printing of this catalog. They include the Lee Gallery; the Department of Art; the Robert J. Rutland Center for Ethics; the Presidential Colloquium program; the Clemson University Vending Committee; and the College of Architecture, Arts and Humanities. Likewise, I am greatly indebted to FURTHERMORE grants in publishing, a program of the J.M. Kaplan Fund, for its support by way of a generous grant for the printing of this catalog.

Deserving special mention are the lenders to the exhibition, listed on a separate page, whose generosity and willingness to share their art works with the Lee Gallery made this exhibition a reality. In this capacity, Mr. Greg Kucera's support of this project is deserving of special acknowledgment. In addition to the paintings that were loaned to us from the Greg Kucera Gallery in Seattle, Mr. Kucera also allowed his gallery facility to serve as the central depository for all paintings collected in the greater Seattle area for inclusion in this exhibition. His staff not only gathered the paintings from the collectors in the greater Seattle area, but also prepared them for shipment to the Lee Gallery here at Clemson University.

My thanks to my colleagues, Denise Woodward-Detrich, Director of the Lee Gallery, and Professor Mike Vatalaro, Interim Chairperson of the Department of Art, for their steadfast support throughout this project's long period of gestation.

I am much indebted to my collaborators, Roger Daniels, Eric Muller, Susan Smith, and Dan Wueste for their informative and stimulating essays; to Krystal Reiko Hauseur for her sensitive and insightful interview with the artist; and to Jessica Barness, former student, for her total and absolute commitment to the design of this catalog. Their varied academic and design backgrounds bring a breadth to the catalog that would otherwise have remained beyond my reach. Their participation and involvement in the development of this catalog are greatly appreciated.

Finally, many thanks to the artist, Roger Shimomura, who gave so freely of his time and assistance throughout the development of this project. Without his generosity this project would not have been possible.

William W Lew
Professor of Art/Art History
Department of Art
Clemson University

Lenders to the Exhibition

Dr. and Mrs. Corey Casper *Seattle, Washington*

Hallie Ford Museum of Art, Willamette University *Salem, Oregon*

Michael and Karen Herman *Kansas City, Missouri*

Catherine Hillenbrand *Seattle, Washington*

Bea Kiyohara *Seattle, Washington*

Greg Kucera Gallery *Seattle, Washington*

The Lawrence Lithography Workshop *Kansas City, Missouri*

Burdett and Michel Loomis *Lawrence, Kansas*

Fred Magenheimer *Long Beach, California*

Dr. and Mrs. Lawrence Y. Matsuda *Seattle, Washington*

Roger Shimomura *Lawrence, Kansas*

Jon and Mary Shirley *Medina, Washington*

Spencer Museum of Art, University of Kansas *Lawrence, Kansas*

Bernice Steinbaum Gallery *Miami, Florida*

Marilyn Domoto Webb *Seattle, Washington*

Anton and Marie Ursini *Chicago, Illinois*

Esther Weissman *Shaker Heights, Ohio*

Driek and Michael Zirinsky *Boise, Idaho*

Minidoka Revisited | Essays

Minidoka Revisited: The Paintings of Roger Shimomura

William W Lew

INTRODUCTION

In 1979 Roger Shimomura completed a series of six large canvases that he eventually titled *Minidoka*. From a stylistic point of view, this series of works appears to be a continuation of an approach that first surfaced in Shimomura's paintings and prints around 1971 and, eventually, became intimately identified with the artist. This approach combines the *ukiyo-e* woodcut styles and images of 18th and 19th century Japan with Pop Art styles and images of the 1960s and the comic book style of Chester Gould (the creator of the Dick Tracy series) into dynamic compositions that exude a "tongue and cheek" humor about his background as an American of Japanese ancestry.

Stylistically, the transition from his earlier works to the *Minidoka* series is seamless. Nevertheless, one cannot help but sense a different set of dynamics at work in the *Minidoka* series—a serious tone and narrative thrust that to date had not been evident in his earlier paintings and prints. The title of this series provides a clue to the more solemn and reflective mood found in these paintings.

Minidoka is now the name of a national monument located in south central Idaho. Shortly after the bombing of Pearl Harbor, however, it served as one of ten relocation centers scattered throughout remote areas of the United States that detained persons of Japanese ancestry then living on the West Coast[1]. Minidoka is the site where approximately 10,000 persons of Japanese ancestry from the Pacific Northwest (including Shimomura and his

1. Minidoka Internment National Monument was established in 2001 as the 385th unit of the National Park System to commemorate the sacrifices of Japanese Americans detained there in the aftermath of Pearl Harbor.

family) were, in fact, incarcerated during the tumultuous years of World War II. Given Shimomura's earlier light-hearted and tongue-in-cheek forays into an art that alluded to his background as a Japanese American, it was merely a matter of time before Shimomura approached related issues of more profound consequence. The *Minidoka* series provided him with an opportunity to do so.

Two important events in 1978 may have triggered and served as the inspirational source for the *Minidoka* series. One of these events was the artist's viewing of a slide presentation in Seattle; the other was his involvement with activities related to the "Day of Remembrance" observance in Puyallup, Washington, a small town located to the south of Seattle. Relative to the slide presentation, an elderly gentlemen named Jack Yamaguchi, who was also a Minidoka internee, had compiled a number of photographic images about life at the relocation center—images that had been excluded from the camp newspaper and had not been shown before. Yamaguchi gave the artist a private showing of these images. The elderly gentleman subsequently developed the series of slides into a slide/tape presentation that over the years has had numerous public showings. It has since become an important document as a visual reminder of life endured in the Minidoka Relocation Center.[2]

Relative to the second event, the "Day of Remembrance" was intended as an occasion of observance and commemoration for those who suffered the Minidoka experience. This event was held on 19 February at the Puyallup fairgrounds, the site that served as the holding camp for the many detainees of Japanese ancestry from Washington before their departure to Minidoka, Idaho.[3] Though recognizing the significance of this event, the artist admitted that his involvement in the 1978 "Day of Remembrance" celebration was limited to the silkscreening of T-shirts for the occasion. However, Shimomura was to play a more significant role in this commemorative occasion in later years.[4]

These two events left an indelible and lasting impression on Shimomura. It was an impression that was to play itself out not only in the artist's *Minidoka* series but also in several series of paintings thereafter.

In recent years, and especially in the aftermath of 9/11, many within the Japanese American community have revisited the "camp experience," questioning whether or not it could happen again—not necessarily to them but to others. Given the pronouncements of such individuals as Howard Coble, U.S. Congressman from North Carolina and Chairman of the Judiciary Subcommittee on Crime, Terrorism and Homeland Security, who stated in a radio program that he agreed with President Franklin D. Roosevelt on the detainment of

2. Jack Yamaguchi's slide/tape presentation was published in book form in 1985 under the title, *This Was Minidoka*. A second edition of this book was printed in 1992.

3. Franklin D. Roosevelt signed Executive Order 9066 on 19 February 1942. Since that first "Day of Remembrance" event on the Puyallup fairgrounds in 1978, this occasion is now observed annually nationwide within the Asian American community, generally on or around 19 February. In 2004, U.S. Representative Michael Honda, from California, introduced a House Resolution supporting "the goals of the Japanese American, German American, and Italian American communities in recognizing a National Day of Remembrance to increase public awareness of the events surrounding the restriction, exclusion, and internment of individuals and families during World War II." This Resolution passed the House by a unanimous vote of 404-0.

4. Shimomura informed me that he not only attended this event several years ago but was one of its speakers.

Japanese Americans in the aftermath of Pearl Harbor, it is no wonder that they have expressed cause for concern. Lest we forget, Shimomura's art admonishes us—sometimes subtly, sometimes veiled in humor and irony, and more recently with a fury and an intensity that strikes us between the eyes like a sharp blow—about our inclinations to succumb to a distrust of those who don't look like us.

I. MINIDOKA—THE JOURNEY

> Minidoka…is a vast stretch of sagebrush stubble and shifting, swirling sand—a dreary, forbidding, flat expanse of arid wilderness. Minidoka, in September of 1942, is the sort of place people would normally traverse only to get through to another destination…
>
> *Minidoka Irrigator*, September 10, 1942[5]

The Minidoka Relocation Center (also known as Hunt) was a 33,000 acre camp situated in the Snake River Plain of south central Idaho. A short distance off Interstate 84, it is located approximately 20 miles northeast of the town of Twin Falls and 15 miles east of the town of Jerome. For years, Shimomura passed by this site as he traveled from Lawrence, Kansas (where he was a member of the faculty at the University of Kansas),[6] to his hometown of Seattle via his van, covering the distance in approximately three to four days. His route was predictable and over the years had become fairly routine—from Lawrence to Denver on Interstate 70; north to Laramie, Wyoming, on Highway 287; west to Ogden, Utah, on Interstate 80; north through Idaho to Hermiston, Oregon, on Interstate 84; north to Ellensburg, Washington, on Interstate 82; and finally west to Seattle on Interstate 90. In the summer of 1983, the artist broke with this routine and took a side trip while in south central Idaho. The sole purpose of this side trip was to visit the site of the Minidoka Relocation Center, his first since the Shimomura family's departure from the camp in which they were incarcerated.[7] This visit took place on the fortieth anniversary of the family's release from the relocation center (and, coincidentally, about four years after Shimomura completed the last of the six paintings that make up his *Minidoka* series). Pilgrimage-like, the artist has seen the necessity to stop at the Minidoka site almost every year since that first summer visit in 1983.

5. Quoted in Robert C. Sims, "Japanese Americans in Idaho," *Japanese Americans: From Relocation to Redress* (Salt Lake City: University of Utah Press, 1986), p. 107.

6. Shimomura joined the Department of Art at the University of Kansas as a member of its faculty in 1969. After 35 years of service at the University of Kansas he retired in 2004 as the department's first Distinguished Professor Emeritus of Art.

7. Shimomura's father was released from the Minidoka Relocation Center in late March 1943 under the auspices of an educational leave and moved to Chicago. Shimomura, his mother, and his sister remained in camp for yet another year and rejoined the father shortly thereafter. Shimomura's grandparents remained yet a third year before uniting with the rest of the family. After a brief stay in Chicago, the entire Shimomura family moved back to Seattle via train from Minneapolis.

II. MINIDOKA—FROM JOURNEY TO PAINTINGS

Although the six paintings have long since found their way into separate collections, this body of works which Shimomura called his *Minidoka* series was originally conceived as a singular entity—the central theme of which was the "camp experience." The series marked Shimomura's earliest major effort into narrative art. Furthermore, the narrative for this series was structured in sequential fashion with each of the six paintings depicting a different phase or aspect of the experience.[8]

On the one hand, the "camp experience" in the series is viewed from a very personal perspective, one that more than hints at the biographical. The content of the works references aspects of the lives of three generations of the Shimomura family. On the other hand, the Shimomura family in these paintings can also be interpreted as a representation of the entire Japanese American community in the Northwest that was incarcerated in the Minidoka Relocation Center.

Minidoka #1 (Notification) and *Minidoka #2 (Exodus)*

In the first of the paintings, *Notification*, the patriarch of the Shimomura family is shown in the foreground reading the notice that abruptly changes the lives of the members of this family (see figure #1, p. 21). Another member of the family, presumably the artist's mother has fallen in a swoon as the grandmother supports and attempts to revive her. The artist, as a young child, is shown clinging to the mother's *kimono*. The second work in this series, entitled *Exodus*, depicts the residents of the Japanese American community in Seattle and its surrounding areas on their forced march to Minidoka (see figure #2, p. 22). The artist presents himself in the foreground, now clinging to his father. Behind the father and son, and to their right, are two figures who appear to be scuffling with each other, apparently differing in their opinions as to how they should respond to the events that have befallen them and that have so painfully impacted their lives. Directly behind these two figures and in the distance is the patriarch of the Shimomura family. He is shown, perhaps in a state of shock and disbelief, as he continues reading the notice.

Before the exodus to Minidoka, members of the Japanese community in Seattle and its surrounding areas were gathered together and relocated on the Western Washington State Fairgrounds in Puyallup, Washington. Puyallup was then an intimate rural community situated halfway between Seattle and Tacoma. The Western Washington Fairgrounds in Puyallup had

8. As previously alluded to, Shimomura's viewing of the Yamaguchi slide presentation may have had a profound influence on the development of his art. Credit may be given to Yamaguchi for Shimomura's foray into a narrative related to the "camp experience." Additionally, the sequential nature of Yamaguchi's slide presentation may also have prompted Shimomura to develop a series of paintings that was also to be viewed in sequential fashion.

FIGURE 1

Minidoka No. 1 (Notification), 1978
Acrylic on Canvas, 60" x 72"
Morgan Family Collection
Kansas City, Missouri

been converted into a temporary assembly center to house its residents before their move to the more permanent relocation center in Hunt, Idaho. The residents remained in this temporary assembly center, called Camp Harmony, for approximately four months before their journey inland via train to Minidoka (see catalog entry #7). In August of 1942, the residents of Camp Harmony finally vacated this temporary assembly center outside of Seattle for the permanent relocation center in Idaho. It is ironic that their journey to Minidoka via

FIGURE 2

Minidoka No. 2 (Exodus), 1978
Acrylic on Canvas, 60" x 72"
Seattle Art Museum

train began at a place called Camp Harmony and concluded in a town called Eden, where they were then bused to the Minidoka Relocation Center. As the first group of detainees stepped off the buses that brought them to their new home, they were greeted by a yet-to-be finished "camp." It is also ironic that a number of the Japanese American detainees were hired by the builders of the camp to erect the barbed wire fence that eventually would enclose them and their families.

22

Minidoka #3 (Diary) and Minidoka #4 (Dream)

The subject matter of the third and fourth works in this series, *Diary* and *Dream*, more specifically focuses on Toku Shimomura, the artist's grandmother (see catalog entries #1 and #2). Unbeknownst to the artist while she was alive, Toku was to play an instrumental role in and to have an overwhelming influence on the development of Shimomura's art. Shimomura's earliest recollections of his grandmother coincided with that period of time when the family was incarcerated at the Minidoka Relocation Center.

In one of the works, the grandmother is shown recording an entry in her diary. Toku faithfully maintained her diaries from the time that she immigrated to this country in 1912 until her death in 1968. With brush in hand, the impressive figure of this person dominates the foreground. The then three-year old Shimomura and his mother are to be seen in the middle ground of this painting, in front of the entranceway to their shelter observing the matron of the Shimomura family engaged in this activity. Beyond the entranceway is a barren landscape with a guard tower and a fence of barbed wire that are barely visible, obscured by clouds of dust.[9]

In the other work Toku is shown with fan in hand, wrapped in a heavy blanket, and seated by a large trunk. She appears to be napping. A large cloud-like shape emits from her head in comic book-like fashion, revealing to us her thoughts while she is in this somnolent state. These thoughts appear to be of happier and bygone times—of family and friends singing, dancing, playing, and, generally, enjoying themselves.

When comparing Shimomura's later works with these two paintings from the *Minidoka* series, we begin to realize the tremendous impact of Toku's influence on the development of this artist. Shimomura's indebtedness to his grandmother cannot be underestimated. And, one would not stray too far off course were one to say that Toku's experiences in this country during the chaotic years of World War II serve as bedrock for Shimomura's art.

Minidoka #5 (442nd) and Minidoka #6 (No-No Boy)

A fierce *samurai* warrior dominates the foreground of the fifth painting in this series, entitled *442nd*—the title's reference is obvious (see figure #3, p.24). This painting commemorates the actions of the 442nd Regimental Combat Team—a segregated combat team comprised of approximately 4,500 Japanese American soldiers that became not only the most highly decorated military unit in World War II, but also in all of U.S. military history. This warrior, with sword and lance in hand, stands before a backdrop of *samurai* figures whose portraits are presented in yearbook-like fashion not unlike that of a high school annual. Indeed, the figures

9. Many of the detainees complained about the ever present dust in the hot summers at Minidoka. We find references to the dust storms in Toku's diaries (see catalog entry #5).

FIGURE 3

Minidoka No. 5 (442nd), 1979
Acrylic on Canvas, 60" x 72"
Tacoma Art Museum

are meant to represent members of this all Japanese American military unit. The main figure is intended to reference the artist's uncle who was one of the members of this unit wounded in the European front. Around this figure's neck is to be seen a sash with the Japanese characters for 4-4-2 emblazoned on it. Under his right armpit and barely visible is to be seen a bloody bandage, covering the wound that he sustained while in battle.

24

The last painting in this series, *No-No Boy*, serves as a sharp counterpoint to the *442nd* both in theme and format (see catalog entry #3). Perhaps the most elusive and enigmatic of the six paintings, *No-No Boy* appears not to relate in any specific way to the circumstances of the Shimomura family. Within the Japanese American community, however, the reference (not unlike 4-4-2) is obvious and well known.

In contrast to those Japanese Americans who supported the wartime effort and who viewed military service as an opportunity to express their patriotism, others were critical of the government's actions—actions that denied them their civil liberties and that imprisoned them and their families within barbed wire compounds located in remote areas of the United States. Their criticisms manifested themselves formally in their response to a four-page questionnaire that was distributed to all draft-age Japanese American males. Intended to explore both their backgrounds and their loyalty to the United States, the questionnaire included two questions that proved to be confusing and particularly offensive to these individuals—questions #27 and #28. The first of these two questions read as follows: "Are you willing to serve in the armed forces of the United States on combat duty, wherever ordered?" The second asked "Will you swear unqualified allegiance to the United States of America and faithfully defend the United States from any or all attack by foreign or domestic forces, and foreswear any form of allegiance or obedience to the Japanese Emperor, or any other foreign government, power, or organization?" Those individuals who responded in the negative to these two questions came to be known as No-No Boys, a disparaging label at best.[10]

Perhaps it was inevitable that tensions would arise between those who volunteered for military service and those who refused—tensions that in some instances developed into animosities and that continue to ripple through the Japanese American community to this day. We are made painfully aware of the stigma attached to this label and of the tensions between the draft resisters and the veterans in a novel of the same name by the Japanese American author, John Okada. Okada's *No-No Boy*, considered to be the first Japanese American novel in the history of American letters, traces the activities of Ichiro, a No-No Boy, after his release from prison and upon his return to his hometown of Seattle where he attempts to resume his life. The setting for much of the novel is Seattle's International District located in the south central part of the city. In the late 1940s, after the war, and in the 1950s, this district included *Nihonmachi* or Japantown and Chinatown. A vibrant focus of Asian American activity it was a district that Shimomura knew well. Okada's novel most likely set the tone and served as the source of inspiration for this particular painting. And, while the

10. Eric L. Muller provides a lucid and insightful analysis of the reinstitution of the Selective Service Procedures for Japanese American males in the wake of events following the bombing of Pearl Harbor in his book, *Free to Die for Their Country: The Story of the Japanese American Draft Resisters in World War II*. See chapter four of this book for a discussion of the issues that prompted the negative responses on the part of the draft resisters.

circumstances of the protagonist in *No-No Boy* are in sharp contrast to those of the artist (who fulfilled his military obligations in the early 1960s), nevertheless, Shimomura feels a strong affinity with the content of this novel; he has referenced Okada on more than one occasion in past conversations.

The *No-No Boy* and *442nd* paintings offer an interesting pairing and a provocative contrast, made more so by the tenuous relationship that exists between the two groups of people that the works allude to. Whether or not Shimomura intended to explore this relationship when he painted the two works in 1979 or to treat the paintings as separate and distinct entities within the context of this series is unclear. Given the position of the Japanese American Citizens League (JACL) in World War II and the number of veterans in the league after the war, however, it is difficult to ignore the tensions that arose between those draftees who willingly served in the 442nd Regimental Combat Team and the No-No Boys. The distance of time has blunted the derisive meaning behind this label. And, while a number of the *Nisei* veterans continue to be bitter, for many of the younger generation in the Japanese American community, the actions of the No-No Boys are looked upon as an act both of conscience and of courage. The actions of these resisters were acknowledged in a public ceremony on 11 May 2002 in which the President of the JACL formally apologized both for the organization's neglect in supporting their protest against injustice and denial of civil rights and for the emotional pain that they endured as a result of this neglect.[11] U.S. Senator Daniel K. Inouye (himself a highly decorated combat veteran of the 442nd Regimental Combat Team) was asked to present the message of reconciliation between the two groups at the ceremony. Because he was unable to attend the ceremony, his message was presented to the audience in attendance via videotape. The following is excerpted from his message:

> I believe the time has come to bridge the chasm between the Nisei veterans of World War II and the resisters from the internment camps. Together we must make a personal commitment to healing the wounds from that sad episode in our collective history.

> If we are to flourish and thrive as a community in this nation, we must put that painful part of our past behind us. I have many friends on both sides of the veterans versus resisters debate. It saddens me that harsh feelings still exit between the veterans and the resisters. I'm especially troubled that people have harbored these bitter feelings for 60 years. We must keep in mind that the volunteers and the resisters had the same goal in mind: to convince our country that it was wrong to imprison Americans of Japanese ancestry...

11. After years of bitter internal debate the resolution calling for this apology was passed at the 2000 JACL biennium national convention, the mandate of which was carried out in the aforementioned public ceremony.

> Many of my fellow veterans have labeled the draft resisters as 'cowards' and 'traitors.' I however feel that the resisters were brave and patriotic. I personally believe it took a tremendous amount of courage and love of country to stand up and say 'I will not take an oath to defend my country until my family and I are treated as equal and worthy citizens…[12]

In contrast to the response that the resisters drew from the JACL and others in the 1940s, the actions of these No-No Boys are now considered to be a benchmark in the annals of U.S. civil rights. What at one time was a stigma has now become a long overdue badge of courage.

On a personal level, Shimomura's *Minidoka* series presents us with a biographical saga of a family attempting as best it can to cope with the travails of an untenable situation in the aftermath of the bombing of Pearl Harbor. On the other hand, and relative to the larger picture, the Shimomura family in this series serves as a personification of the collective Japanese American spirit during the trying times of World War II.

As alluded to throughout, Shimomura presents the subject matter in his *Minidoka* series vis-à-vis the guise of the *ukiyo-e* traditions of 18th and 19th century Japanese art. One might interpret the use of these styles as a means to give the events depicted a uniquely Japanese American frame of reference—a Japanese American artistic sensibility. And, perhaps, there is a degree of substance to such an interpretation. However, what is to differentiate "Japanese" from "Japanese American?" That viewers might also mistake the works for traditional Japanese paintings and perhaps miss their "message" entirely was a concern that was not only anticipated by the artist but also intended on his part. Past experience had alerted him to the stereotyping that goes on for U.S. citizens who, like Shimomura, look foreign. How often had he, himself, been mistaken for a Japanese who spoke "good" English rather than for a third generation American citizen whose native tongue was English. Shimomura found this to be true in art as well as in life.

> …people that were seeing my paintings thought them to be a homecoming of sorts. In other words, I now painted that way because, to them, I have always looked that way. Little did they realize how foreign-appearing, to me, the geisha and samurai were in my compositions. These were not the images around me while growing up; these were the exotic things I associated with my grandparents and the images in their scrapbooks. This became my first contact with the notion of irony.[13]

One cannot underestimate the sometimes subtle, sometimes blatant role of irony in Shimomura's art. In reference to the *Diary* series (begun shortly after the completion of

12. Martha Nakagawa, "Historic Apology Marks First Step in Reconcilation Between JACL and Resisters of Conscience," Pacific Citizen, May 17-June 6, 2002, http://www.resisters.com/news/apology_pc.htm, 20 March 2005.

13. Roger Shimomura, "The 63 Stages of the Yellow Brick Road," keynote address presented at the College Art Association (CAA) Annual Conference, New York City, February 2003, http://www.collegeart.org/caa/news/2003/May/RogerShimomura.html, 12 March 2004.

the *Minidoka* series) Shimomura stated, "I consciously kept the camp paintings in the *ukiyo-e* style, with the diary-entry subjects buried within them as a subtext to the superficial decorative appearance of the work, similar to applying perfumed deodorant over a bad case of body odor."[14] The same can be said for the six paintings that make up Shimomura's *Minidoka* series.

III. TOKU'S DIARIES

Toku Shimomura, through her diaries, was to exert a tremendous influence on Shimomura's art. And we should view the *Diary* painting from the *Minidoka* series as an important and prophetic work relative to Shimomura's development as an artist. As previously mentioned, Toku Shimomura, is shown in the foreground with brush in hand, about to jot an entry into her diary. The mother who is holding the artist as a young toddler is located in the middle ground of the painting in front of the entranceway to their household at the Minidoka Relocation Center.

Shimomura's grandmother emigrated from Japan to the United States early in the second decade of the 20th century, in 1912. Even before her move to this country, she recorded her rounds of daily activities in diaries that appear to have been an important part of her daily life. According to Shimomura, she faithfully maintained her diary activities up to the time of her death in the late 1960s. He recalls giving his grandmother blank or new diaries as gifts during the Christmas season. After her death, the artist inherited his grandmother's diaries.

The artist discovered that his grandmother recorded her diary entries in Japanese. Being a *Sansei* (third generation American of Japanese ancestry) and having no knowledge of the written Japanese language, Shimomura applied for and received a research grant at the University of Kansas to have the diary entries translated for him. The diaries, however, contained decades worth of entries, and one question confronting the artist was where to begin the translations. Because Shimomura's earliest cognizance of his grandmother was in the early 1940s when he and his family were incarcerated at Minidoka, he decided to begin the translation project with those entries that corresponded to his earliest remembrance of his grandmother.

IV. THE *DIARY* AND *AMERICAN DIARY* SERIES

On a personal level, the translations of these entries provided Shimomura with insights both about his grandmother and of life in the Minidoka Relocation Center. More importantly for our understanding of Shimomura's development as an artist, the translations served (and continue to serve) as a source of inspiration for his paintings and as an important aspect of the artist's creative modus operandi. Indeed, diary entries related to the "camp" experience and to events leading to the incarceration of the Shimomura family at the Minidoka Relocation Center serve as foci for the works that comprise the artist's *Diary* and *American Diary* series, respectively painted in the 1980s and the 1990s.

In both his *Diary* and *American Diary* series, the artist used events related to specific diary entries as the reference points and primary themes for the individual paintings that make up these two groups of works. For example, the diary entry for the day on which Pearl Harbor was attacked reads as follows:

> When I came back from church today, I heard the dreamlike news that Japanese airplanes had bombed Hawaii. I was shocked beyond belief. I sat in front of the radio and listened to the news all day. They said that at 6 a.m. Japan declared war on the United States. Our future has become gloomy. I pray that God will stay with us.

In response to the diary entry dated December 7, 1941, the artist painted an image of his grandmother before a radio, listening and responding in horror to the sad news about the bombing of Pearl Harbor (see catalog entry #4). Consistent with the *Diary* painting from his *Minidoka* series, Toku is presented in a 19th century Japanese woodcut style. The radio that is partially obscured by Toku, however, reveals a style that is more akin to art deco.[15] The juxtaposition and overlaying of disparate artistic styles and objects becomes a hallmark of Shimomura's personal style in the *Diary* series and many of his other paintings.

It is also important to note that the entries not only serve as themes for the paintings that comprise these two series but also as important complements to the works themselves. The translations of these diary entries generally are included on the information placards and labels that accompany and identify the works when the paintings are on exhibit.

Shimomura often revisits and finds new inspiration in diary entries that had been used in previous paintings. It is not unusual for the artist to paint several versions of a work based on the same diary entry. Such is the case with the aforementioned *Diary: Dec 7, 1941*, painting.

15. The model for this radio was to be found in Shimomura's collection of art deco radios. It and others from his collection of radios served as models for other versions of his "Dec 7, 1941" painting (three other versions in the *Diary* series and one version in the *American Diary* series). Shimomura is a collector of objects. His forays into collecting began with his acquisition of art deco radios. The interaction between his art and his various collections is the topic of another study under consideration.

16. This series of works including both paintings and prints, was organized by the Smithsonian Institution and shown at a number of major museums nationwide between 1998 and 2002. In 2001 the College Art Association recognized this series of works and honored Shimomura with its *Artist Award for Most Distinguished Body of Works*.

This work, in fact, is the third version of four paintings inspired by the entry that was entered into Toku's diaries on December 7, 1941.

Some of the entries that serve as sources of inspiration for works in the *Diary* series also find their way into Shimomura's *American Diary* series.[16] However, it is instructive to note that the works in the *American Diary* series abandon the eighteenth and nineteenth century Japanese woodcut styles that played such a prominent role in the earlier *Minidoka* and *Diary* series. The *American Diary* series, which dates from 1997, was painted under the auspices of and with support from a Civil Liberties Public Education Fund (CLPEF) grant. According to the artist, this Fund was supported by reparation monies that had been set aside to educate the public on the internment experience. Noting the greater emphasis on the didactic function of this series, Shimomura chose to employ a more direct approach to the depiction of his subject matter. The sharp contrast in styles can be noted in a comparison of the paintings entitled, *Diary: August 27, 1942*, and *American Diary: May 16, 1942 (Camp Harmony)* (see catalog entries #5 and #7). In the latter, the artist reverts back to a more straightforward comic book narrative style that is first seen in his works in the late 1960s and very early 1970s.

As is suggested in the above, the translations of specific diary entries serve both as the source of inspiration and as an aspect of Shimomura's creative modus operandi for these paintings. The use of written narrative as an important complement to visual images is also to be seen in a series of paintings that the artist completed in 2004. However, the narratives, while dealing with issues of concern to the Asian American community, are no longer based on entries from the grandmother's diaries. This series, entitled, *Stereotypes and Admonitions*, draws upon incidents of racial insensitivity that Shimomura has both observed within the larger Asian American community and experienced personally within his own lifetime. Not unlike the *Diary* and *American Diary* series, the written narrative, which describes a specific event, is intended as an instrumental component of the artwork that was inspired by it.

Stylistically, this body of works reveals a kinship to both the *Diary* and *American Diary* series in that the paintings that make up this series also employ the aforementioned *ukiyo-e* and comic book style. However, the subject matter in many of the works in this more recent series appears to be much more aggressively rendered, due, perhaps, to the nature of the issues that they confront (see catalog entries #14, #20, #23).

V. STEREOTYPES

In 2003 the artist was the recipient of a Joan Mitchell Painting Award, one of only ten artists in the United States to receive this prestigious award that year. The award provided Shimomura with the time and the resources to continue with and to elaborate on a series of works that first took form in the preceding year and that dealt specifically with issues of ethnic/racial stereotyping. Entitled, *Stereotypes and Admonitions,* and consisting of a total of thirty paintings, this body of works has had several showings in progressive phases of its development from 2002 to 2004. The first ten paintings from this series were shown in an exhibition in Miami, Florida. A second showing, including an additional ten works, was presented in Kansas City, Missouri. Finally, all thirty works were presented in a major showing in Seattle, Washington, in 2004.[17]

The *Stereotypes and Admonitions* series reveals a collage of artistic styles that have now become intimately identified with Shimomura. These include the style of the Japanese *ukiyo-e* traditions found in the earlier *Minidoka* and *Diary* series, the more straightforward cartoon style that we find in the *American Diary* series, and, now, a more outwardly strident cartoon characterization of the Japanese male. Relative to the latter, the artist has taken off his gloves and has confronted his viewing audience directly and, perhaps, in a confrontational way relative to racial stereotypes. It is as if Shimomura has done away with the "perfumed deodorant" in his paintings and has allowed that "bad case of body odor" to hit our nostrils full force.

In these paintings the Japanese male (and by extension other Asian males) is generally depicted as a round—or broad-faced, yellow-skinned, slant-eyed, buck-toothed, sometimes bespectacled figure that is a demeaning stereotype at best. It is a demeaning cartoon stereotype that is not totally of Shimomura's imagination, but one that originates in caricatures of Asians that date back to World War II and earlier. An inveterate collector of objects that depict Asian stereotypes, Shimomura may have found his prototype for this image in one of the items in his collections. Among his collectibles are pop-up targets that were used by the U.S. military in World War II for rifle practice. On these targets are depicted cartoon heads of an Asian male whose description fits that of the above. Interestingly enough, in the early 1960s when Shimomura was fulfilling his military obligations in Korea, his fellow white officers nicknamed him "Pop-up" because they thought he looked like the image on those targets with which they practiced.[18] Apparently, the military did not distinguish the differences

17. The Bernice Steinbaum Gallery in Miami first introduced this series to the public in 2002. The Jan Weiner Gallery in Kansas City organized the midwest showing of this series. In 2004, the Greg Kucera Gallery in Seattle provided the artist with a major showing of this body of works. The exhibition at the Kucera Gallery was accompanied by a fully illustrated and informative catalog.

18. Shimomura, "The 63 Stages of the Yellow Brick Road."

between the Japanese and the Koreans in those targets. Neither did Shimomura's colleagues and fellow officers make any distinctions.

This image which plays such a prominent role in a number of the paintings in the *Stereotypes and Admonitions* series actually served as the dominant theme and focus for another set of paintings that the artist completed in 2001. In this earlier series, entitled, *Jap's a Jap*, Shimomura introduces this image into his work for the first time (see catalog entry #8). The image is shown clothed in Western attire and placed in a "white man's world" that is reminiscent of the old Walt Disney and Archie and Veronica comic books. According to the artist, this strange juxtaposition is meant to "…represent a reality for many Asian Americans—that not a day goes by when they are not in some way, reminded how they are perceived as being different from the people around them." That perception certainly influenced the titling of this set of paintings and impacted other works produced by the artist in this period of time—the prime example being his *How to Tell the Difference Between the Japanese and the Chinese.*

The title of this series, *Jap's a Jap*, is a reference once again to the incarceration of persons of Japanese ancestry during World War II. In this instance, Shimomura draws upon the words of Lieutenant General John DeWitt, who in 1942 was Franklin D. Roosevelt's head of the Western Defense Command and the person who spearheaded the movement to evacuate and incarcerate both Japanese aliens and Japanese Americans living on the West Coast. On more than one occasion, DeWitt made the following pronouncement: "A Jap's a Jap. It makes no difference whether the Jap is a citizen or not."[19] DeWitt certainly was not a lone voice in his expression of such a sentiment. The news media in California followed suit. The *Los Angeles Times* in its condemnation of the Japanese living on the West Coast expressed the following: "A viper is nonetheless a viper wherever the egg is hatched—so a Japanese American, born of Japanese parents—grows up to be a Japanese, not an American."[20] While DeWitt and other like-minded individuals refused to acknowledge the difference between native-born and American-born Japanese in the chaotic times following Pearl Harbor, there are yet many today who seem unable to get beyond physical appearances and to recognize the fact that a person of Asian ancestry might even be a third generation American. Shimomura reminds us of those occasions in the incidences depicted in his *The History of Art* (see catalog entry #18), *Florence, South Carolina* (see catalog entry #15), and *Do You Speak English* (see catalog entry #14).

19. The first of these pronouncements, which is quoted in the text, was made in 1942. In (13 April) 1943, before the U.S. House of Representatives Naval Affairs Subcommittee, DeWitt stated again that "A Jap's a Jap," and went on to say "They are a dangerous element, whether loyal or not. There is no way to determine their loyalty…it makes no difference whether he is an American; theoretically, he is still a Japanese and you can't change him…You can't change him by giving him a piece of paper."

20. Quote in Ronald Takaki, *A Different Mirror: A History of Multicultural America* (Boston, Toronto, London: Little, Brown and Company), p. 380.

Generalizations based primarily on physical appearances, as alluded to in the aforementioned paintings, also lead to other mistaken notions about ethnicity and race. And, Shimomura is quick to point this out in his *How to Tell the Difference Between the Japanese and the Chinese* (see catalog entry #9). Also called *Yellow Rat Bastard,* this work plays on yet another ethnic/racial cliché about misidentification—that all Asians look alike. The work is a diptych that references himself (Japanese American) in one of the panels and Norman Gee (Chinese American), a close friend and colleague on the painting faculty in the Department of Art at the University of Kansas, in the other panel. Among the profusion of images to be found in the diptych are racist symbols. The round- or broad-faced, yellow-skinned, slant-eyed, buck-toothed, sometimes bespectacled figure that is the subject of the artist's *Jap's a Jap* series is to be seen behind and almost obscured by Shimomura's portrait. Likewise, an image of Fu Manchu, the Chinese villain of World War II, is almost totally obscured by Gee's portrait. Though hidden, the associations are not lost to us; Shimomura does not allow us to dismiss such associations. The two panels are separated by a pedestal that is crowned by a set of Mickey Mouse ears from which hangs a shopping bag with the words "Yellow Rat Bastard." The artist actually found the shopping bag at a trendy "hip hop" clothing store bearing the same name in the SOHO district of New York City. An ethnic/racial slur used to describe the Japanese in World War II, "Yellow Rat Bastard" emerges in the 21st century as a brand name and commercial commodity at the expense of the Asian American community. Shimomura also draws our attention to similar commercial insensitivity in his painting entitled, *Abercrombie & Fitch* (see catalog entry #11).

In 2002 the company, Abercrombie & Fitch, introduced a line of T-shirts that disparaged persons of Asian ancestry and drew the ire of the Asian American community. The company withdrew this line of clothing shortly after it received complaints and criticisms from various Asian American groups. According to Shimomura, a spokesperson for Abercrombie & Fitch stated that "the company felt the shirts would be especially loved by the Asian American community and would be seen as cheeky, irreverent and funny. He was surprised by the hostile reception the merchandise received."[21]

In the aftermath of September 11, 2001, the Anton Gallery in Washington, D.C., organized an invitational exhibition, the theme of which revolved around how artists responded to this tragic event. Shimomura was one of the artists invited to participate in this exhibition. Like many Japanese Americans who endured the "camp experience" of World War II, the tragic events of 9/11 immediately called to mind December 7, 1941. According to the artist: "The

21. See *Roger Shimomura Stereotypes and Admonitions* exh. cat. (Seattle, WA: Greg Kucera Gallery, 2004)

comparison to Pearl Harbor is what hit home. It was like rerunning an old movie.... So I immediately thought of this story and thought of those of Arab or Middle Eastern extraction in this country. It's part of the story of that day."[22] The painting that resulted from these reflections includes an image of a turbaned, mustached and bearded Middle Easterner. Interestingly enough, the image—much in the manner of the stereotyped Asian male—is also slant-eyed, buck-toothed, and yellow-skinned. In the background, partially obscured by this figure and cropped by the outer edges of the painting is to be seen an airplane which bears a remarkable resemblance to a stylized Japanese Zero. The comparison is intentionally unmistakable.

This comparison is made once again in a work from the artist's *Stereotypes and Admonitions* series entitled, *Not Pearl Harbor* (see catalog entry #23). Shimomura also uses this image as a self-portrait in another work that is entitled, *Iran Hostage Crisis* (see catalog entry #20). The work references an incident when the artist was forced off a road by a pickup truck. The narrative which serves as the caption for and complements this painting is self-explanatory and reads as follows:

> During the Iran Hostage Crisis of 1987, Roger was jogging on a country road approximately a mile from his house when a pickup truck carrying two men approached. When the truck got within 50 feet, it suddenly veered toward him, causing Roger to jump into a gully beside the road. As Roger leapt from the road the driver leaned out the window and flipped Roger his middle finger, yelling as he sped off, "That's for your ayatollah, you Chinaman!"[23]

Here, the demographics of misidentification extend beyond the Asian American community to encompass that of the Mid-East as well.

Anxieties within the Asian American community resulting from the comparison between the events of September 11, 2001, and December 7, 1941, changed to outrage as a result of comments by Howard Coble, U.S. Congressman from North Carolina and the Chairman of the Judiciary Subcommittee on Crime, Terrorism and Homeland Security (see catalog entry #21). In a radio call-in program about national security that was aired on February 4, 2003, in Greensboro, North Carolina, a caller suggested that Arabs in the U.S. should be sent to internment camps during the war on terrorism. Coble disagreed with the caller. He, however, went on to remark that he did agree with FDR's decision to intern persons of Japanese ancestry during World War II and believed that the decision was right. Later he commented that it

22. Jan Biles, "Date Looms Large in Artwork," *Lawrence Journal World*, September 11, 2002, http://www2.ljworld.com/news/2002/sep/11/date_looms_large/, 22 August 2005.

23. *See Roger Shimomura Stereotypes and Admonitions* exh. cat. (Seattle, WA: Greg Kucera Gallery, 2004).

had not just to do with national security but was also intended to ensure the safety of the Japanese Americans.

In reaction to these comments by Coble, Roy H. Saigo, President of St. Cloud University in Minneapolis, Minnesota, and himself a former internee, prepared an article that appeared in the newspaper, *The Charlotte Observer*. In the article Saigo stated:

> Earlier this month, Rep. Howard Coble, R-N.C., made a grossly offensive statement. He said that the World War II internment camps for Japanese Americans were justified because people of Japanese descent were "an endangered species" who needed protection. I was in one of those concentration camps between the ages of 2 and 5, along with my parents, my siblings and 120,000 others who looked like us. If we were there for our own protection, as Coble suggested, why were the machine guns on the outside pointed in, along with the barbed wire on the fences?[24]

The question posed by Saigo proves to be a constant in Shimomura's *Minidoka*, *Diary* and *American Diary* series, and in his *Justified Internment* painting. Barbed wire and guard towers are certainly meant as important visual subtexts in these series, occurring and recurring from one work to another. That these elements are interpreted by some viewers merely as decorative motifs and nothing more was made very apparent to the artist in several responses that he received relative to the last of the paintings in his *Diary* series. According to the artist, three persons were interested in purchasing the painting, however, only under the condition that he paint out the barbed wire in the background of the work.[25] Suffice it to say that not a one of these individuals purchased the painting. We can only hope that Saigo's question is not as easily and summarily dismissed by the American audience as the barbed wire was by the three prospective purchasers of Shimomura's painting.

VI. POSTSCRIPT

> Those who do not remember the past are condemned to repeat it.　　　George Santayana

> …I must admit to being concerned about the loss of momentum of political work [art], for I believe in the kind of vibrancy that social conscience breeds, and I believe in the richness that sharing of life stories and experiences bring to the world as a whole.
>
> 　　　　　　　　　　　　　　　　　　　Roger Shimomura

24. Roy Hirofumi Saigo, "Congressman's remarks bring back bad memories of internment," *The Charlotte Observer*, February 28, 2003, p. 13A.

25. Shimomura, "The 63 Stages of the Yellow Brick Road."

As Roger Shimomura informs us in his paintings, art and politics make for interesting and important bedfellows. The relationship between the two have both dogged and inspired Shimomura for three and a half decades, going back to an incident in 1971 when a farmer in Lawrence, Kansas, upon meeting the artist, would only see a person from Japan who spoke "good" English standing before him. According to Shimomura, the exchange between the two "changed my work and life forever." Who Shimomura was, where he came from, and how he was viewed by others became a driving force in his work. This force gained new momentum and meaning for Shimomura in 1978 when he embarked on his *Minidoka* series and the subsequent series that interpreted the "camp" experience through the person of Toku Shimomura, his grandmother. Biographical on one level, Shimomura's work can also be viewed as the expression of a collective Asian American conscience that continually and unfortunately needs to mediate and reconcile its presence in this country.

I am reminded of a reference that Shimomura made in his 2003 keynote presentation at the National College Art Association Conference in New York City. The reference was directed at the comments of an art critic who wrote that "the public has tired of seeing images of victimization, and that it is time to move on, to move outside of the social-cause ghettos that have been created." Shimomura went on to state that the critic considered these kinds of issues merely as "social constructs or ideas about racism that have lost their vitality, that were now out of fashion and that have been "ghettoized."[26] In a very similar vein, I am also reminded of Shimomura's painting, *Passé*, which references a proposal that the artist presented for a public art project (see catalog entry #24). The narrative that accompanies and complements this painting informs us that Shimomura lost the commission for this project because an art historian on the selection panel thought that the theme dealing with multicultural issues in this country was "soooo passé." Let us all be grateful that the art critic and the art historian have not persuaded Roger Shimomura to paint out the barbed wire in his work.

26. Shimomura, "The 63 Stages of the Yellow Brick Road."

36

Ethnic Cleansing in America?
The Mass Incarceration of Japanese Americans, 1942-46

Roger Daniels

According to the Census of 1940 there were 126,948 Japanese Americans living in the continental United States. Two years later 110,000 of them were incarcerated in ten bleak, barbed-wire-ringed camps in the remoter parts of California, Idaho, Arizona, Utah, Wyoming, Colorado, and Arkansas. In the process the state of California, the western halves of Washington and Oregon, and a portion of Arizona, were cleared of persons of Japanese birth or ancestry except for a few dozen who were institutionalized.

Some 70 percent of those prisoners without trial were native-born citizens of the United States. At the time the government used a variety of euphemisms to describe this imprisonment, the most common of which were "evacuation" and "relocation."[1] It seems to me now, in 2005, that the term "ethnic cleansing," which was not coined until the Balkan wars of the 1990s, is perhaps most appropriate, not only for what happened to Japanese Americans but also for what was done to American tribal peoples as they were moved progressively westward in the eighteenth and nineteenth centuries.

President Franklin D. Roosevelt proposed to Secretary of the Interior Harold L. Ickes in June 1944 that some Japanese Americans eventually be allowed to return to the Pacific Coast and that in the rest of the country they be distributed so that only one or two families would be resettled in any one county.

There is also the related question of what to call the camps themselves. The government called them "relocation centers," most Japanese Americans came to call them simply "camps," but many scholars and activists call them "concentration camps," a term which Roosevelt, their ultimate creator, used on more than one public occasion. In later years many

1. I have discussed this issue in "Words Do Matter: A Note on Inappropriate Terminology and the Incarceration of the Japanese Americans," pp. 190-214, in Louis Fiset and Gail M. Nomura, eds. Nikkei in the Pacific Northwest. (Seattle: University of Washington Press, 2005), but written several years earlier.

shunned that term because of its connotation of mass murder as in the camps of the Third Reich or the Soviet Union. Somehow the phrase "the internment of the Japanese Americans" became all but universally used.

While there can be debate about the right word for the camps, "internment" is clearly the wrong word. In both American and international law internment describes the process by which both the civilian nationals and combatants of one warring power in the custody of another power may be confined. Many nations, including the United States, had subscribed to a protocol, known as the Geneva Convention, which governed the treatment of both kinds of internees.

Accordingly, the United States, as it had done in previous wars, set up internment camps, under the jurisdiction of the Department of Justice, in which, even before the United States was at war, sailors from German and Italian ships which sought safety in American ports were interned. After the United States was actually at war in December 1941, Roosevelt signed a series of proclamations based on existing statute law which made all Japanese, German, and Italian nationals 14 years of age and older "alien enemies" and liable to be "apprehended, restrained, secured, and removed." There were nearly a million such persons in the continental United States—some 600,000 Italians, 300,000 Germans, and 50,000 Japanese. The government had no intention of taking that many people into custody and during the entire war only about 12,000 such persons were interned, some 8,000 Japanese, 3,000 Germans, and a few hundred Italians.

Most of those arrested were community leaders whose real or imagined ties to their home governments had caused them to be placed on various government watch lists. As part of the internment process, all those arrested for internment were entitled to hearings, which resulted, in some cases, in release without internment. Many if not most of those interned were probably harmless to the United States, but there was at least a putative probable cause for their internment.

As December turned into January and the dimensions of the continuing American military disaster in the Pacific became more and more apparent, American politicians, the news media, and some military officials created escalating demand for the federal government to do something about all the Japanese on the West Coast. Demands from Congress, supported by Secretary of War Henry L. Stimson, an establishment Republican who had been brought into Roosevelt's cabinet as a unity gesture after the fall of France in 1940, eventually led President Roosevelt to issue Executive Order 9066 on February 19, 1942, which, in effect, empowered the United States Army to remove all persons of Japanese ancestry from the entire state of California, the coastal portions of Oregon and Washington, the entire territory of Alaska, and a small portion of Arizona. Japanese Americans living elsewhere in the continental United States were left in nervous liberty throughout the war.

Four decades later the reasons for this decision were analyzed by the presidential Commission on Wartime Relocation and Internment of Civilians (CWRIC):

> The promulgation of Executive Order 9066 was not justified by military necessity...The broad historical causes...were race prejudice, war hysteria, and a failure of political leadership. Widespread ignorance of Japanese Americans contributed to a policy conceived in haste and executed in an atmosphere of fear and anger at Japan. A grave injustice was done to Americans and resident aliens of Japanese ancestry, who without any individual review or probative evidence against them, were excluded, removed and detained by the United States during World War II. (Personal Justice Denied, p.18)

Although the general in charge, Lt. Gen. John L. DeWitt had predicted that it would be a simple task to round up the West Coast Japanese Americans, moving them to the Assembly Centers—located fairly close to their homes—did not begin until the end of March, and the movements to the permanent Relocation Centers were not completed until October 31, 1942.

The Army ran the Assembly Centers and its Corps of Engineers was responsible for building the Relocation Centers. With sub-rosa help from a demographer on loan from the Census Bureau, the Army divided the West Coast into 108 districts and issued a separate Civilian Exclusion Order (CEO) to cover each one. Rather than try to describe each of the sixteen Assembly Centers and ten Relocation Centers, this essay will trace briefly the "progress" of one family from freedom to captivity and eventual release. Like the rest of the incarcerated people, its members were charged with no crime. Their fate was determined by their ancestry and where they were living in the early spring of 1942.

The members of the Shimomura family of Seattle (father Kazuo Eddie Shimomura, 29 years old, his wife, Aya, aged 23, and son Yutaka Roger, who was almost three years old—all American citizens) were moved fairly early in the process as they fell under CEO #17 and were forced from their home at the end of April 1942. That order had been posted conspicuously throughout their neighborhood on April 24, informing "all persons of Japanese ancestry, both alien and non-alien" that they were being excluded and that one member of each family was to report to a designated neighborhood control point April 25 (see figure #1, p. 21 and catalog entry #6). Each family got a number. The Shimomura family was #10,801. During their shipment each family member had to wear a tag bearing that number. On April 30 and May 1 the Shimomuras and nearly 1,200 of their neighbors were transported to the Western Washington State Fairgrounds in nearby Puyallup (catalog entry #7). They could bring with them only what they could carry. All other possessions had to be stored or disposed of at their own expense.[2]

When the exiled families reached the Fairgrounds they found that they were in a large cage ringed with barbed wire and guard towers manned by armed soldiers whose guns were pointed inward. The Shimomuras, along with 7,600 others, would live in that cage through the rest of the spring and summer. They were assigned quarters in what had been the parking lot: they were housed in one of scores of jerry-built wooden barracks 120 feet long by 20 feet wide divided into seven one-room "apartments," each lighted by a bare light bulb hanging from the ceiling. There was no running water. Wood stoves provided heating. There was one window at the back wall of each unit facing a solid front door. All ate in mess halls designed to feed 500 persons three meals a day and used grouped toilets and showers that were segregated by gender but otherwise offered no privacy.

In the fall the inmates of Puyallup were moved in increments by train to a "permanent" camp called Minidoka in southern Idaho, where 9,397 persons were detained. Accommodations there were similar to those at Puyallup, but slightly larger. A civilian agency, the War Relocation Authority (WRA), was created to administer the camps and regulate the lives of the inmates, but Army-controlled military police units provided security, with the now familiar guard towers punctuating the barbed wire. The WRA tried to turn each of the ten Relocation Centers into a small city. Each was provided with a hospital, schools, a newspaper, a post office, and a cooperatively run canteen where small purchases could be made. Most of what would have been civil service and professional jobs in the outside world were taken by inmates who could receive a maximum pay of $19 a month. Top administrators, some teachers and medical personnel were non-inmates, almost all Caucasian, were paid federal wage rates.

Once they were under WRA authority it became possible for the prisoners to leave camp to shop in the nearest town. Able-bodied men and women were allowed to take approved temporary jobs outside of camp, mostly as agricultural laborers, but were supposed to return after the harvest was over. The WRA also established a system it called "leave clearance" but which was all but tantamount to release.

The three possible reasons for leave were for military service, work, or education. Among the first to leave were men with a working knowledge of Japanese who enlisted in the Army's Military Intelligence Service. News of their service, which might have helped the national image of Japanese Americans, was kept secret until after the war. Among other early leavers were some college students who were allowed to attend those schools east of the Rockies which would accept them. All who left—except for those recruited by Army Intelligence—had to pass loyalty checks conducted by the FBI.

Hoping to regularize and ease this process, the WRA decided to determine loyalty en masse by means of a questionnaire distributed to all inmates, male and female, citizen and alien. Instead of constructing its own questionnaire—the WRA employed a number of social scientists—administrators used one developed by the Army for aliens who were willing to enlist.

Before the WRA questionnaire was issued, the Army announced on January 28, 1943, that it would form an all-*Nisei* combat team and called for volunteers. The draft had been ended for Japanese Americans in early 1942; they were put in category 4-C, normally reserved for enemy aliens. In addition, many, but not all Japanese Americans who had been drafted after October 1940 had been summarily discharged. Naturally there was great debate by young men and their families about whether volunteering was appropriate given the treatment they had received.

Less than two weeks later, on February 10, the WRA issued its questionnaire, which was titled "Application for Leave Clearance." This created more confusion as many elderly *Issei* did not want to leave the camps. The crucial questions were questions 27 and 28.

No. 27. Are you willing to serve in the armed forces of the United States on combat duty, wherever ordered?

No. 28. Will you swear unqualified allegiance to the United States of America and faithfully defend the United States from any and all attack by foreign or domestic forces, and forswear any form of allegiance or obedience to the Japanese emperor, to any other foreign potentate, power or organization?

What aged *Issei* or women of any age were to make of question 27 is hard to say, but question 28 was even worse. For the Issei, who were, under American law, ineligible for naturalization because of their race, it meant voluntarily assuming stateless status. In addition it was a violation of the Geneva Convention to ask them to do so. Eventually the WRA changed the question for them to:

> Will you swear to abide by the laws of the United States and to take no action which would in any way interfere with the war effort of the United States?

The adult Shimomuras, like a large majority of the incarcerated people, answered "yes" to both questions and thus were eligible for early release. On March 22, 1943, the elder Shimomura left on indefinite educational leave for Chicago. His wife did not join him until mid-April 1944, and brought with her young Roger and his new sister, Hisako Carolyn, who had been born in the camp hospital on August 15, 1943, one of 5,918 Americans born in wartime captivity.

Most Japanese American inmates spent longer in camp. Minidoka was not emptied until October 1945 and the last camp operated until March 1946. Some Japanese Americans never left: 1,862 died in captivity, all but a very few of natural causes. There were a number of suicides and at three of the camps —Manzanar, Topaz, and Tule Lake—there were confrontations in which young American soldiers shot and killed several young Japanese Americans. No one was ever punished for any of these deaths.

For decades after 1945 the wartime incarceration was all but ignored by most Americans and even most Japanese Americans said little about it publicly or even to their postwar children. This began to change in the 1960s, largely through the efforts of some of those children of the third or *Sansei* generation, who, like other Americans in those years were wont to question authority. In 1976, during the Bicentennial celebrations, President Gerald R. Ford revoked Roosevelt's 1942 Executive Order 9066, declaring in the process:

> We now know what we should have known then – not only was [the] evacuation wrong, but Japanese-Americans were and are loyal Americans.

Four years later Congress passed and President Jimmy Carter signed the law establishing the CWRIC whose report, quoted above, was issued on February 24, 1983. It later recommended that the government issue a formal apology and pay each survivor a one-time tax-free payment of $20,000. After five years of debate Congress passed and Ronald Reagan signed the Civil Liberties Act which effected the CWRIC's recommendation. No payments were made until October 1990 and payments continued well into the decade. Letters of apology were signed by two presidents, George H. Bush and Bill Clinton.

The whole process of what Japanese Americans call redress helped to make many Americans aware of what Japanese Americans had suffered during World War II. This became clear in the wake of the tragic event we have learned to call 9/11. When the government began to round up thousands of ethnic suspects, almost all of whom were resident aliens, comparison with the events of 1941-42 was raised not only by protesters but also at the highest levels of government (see catalog entry #23). In the subsequent months there were many more protests about the treatment of just several thousand persons than there had been about the treatment of Japanese Americans during the four-year Pacific War. A six-decade reflection on the Japanese American experience surely was at least partly responsible for the relative mildness of the government's reaction to the terrorist attack, although there were many examples of "prejudice, war hysteria, and a failure of political leadership."

Some Comments by a Law Professor

Eric L. Muller

I am delighted to have been asked to contribute some thoughts to this program for *Minidoka Revisited*, this exhibit of some of the work of Roger Shimomura. Several years ago, Roger graciously offered me the use of one of his works in connection with a book I was writing about Japanese American internees who resisted the military draft during World War II. I am very happy to be able to repay his kindness and generosity.

I am a law professor, and therefore cannot avoid approaching the story of the Japanese American internment, at least in part, from the perspective of the law. The greatest goals of the law are, of course, to advance the cause of fairness and to prevent grave injustices. But the law's method is subtle, more interested in investigating shades of difference than in painting stark contrasts. The common law method we inherited from England is a practice of comparing the facts of this new case with the facts of that old one, to determine whether the two are sufficiently alike to apply the old rule, or whether slight differences between the two cases counsel either the modification of the old rule or the application of a different rule entirely. It is an exercise in close comparison and nuanced deliberation.

Thus, the first thing that I notice in Roger's work about the Japanese American experience in World War II is its starkness and exaggeration. I speak here of the almost comic-book style of representation that Roger often uses, and his penchant for depicting his subjects with the attributes of caricature and even stereotype. Consider, for example, the piece entitled *Minidoka #5 (442nd)*, which depicts members of the justly famed 442nd Regimental Combat Team (see figure #3, p. 24). The 442nd, or "the four-four-two," as its veterans call it, was the racially segregated battalion that the U.S. Army created in 1943 for Japanese American soldiers. The 442nd fought with incredible valor in the European Theater from late 1943 through war's end, garnering more decorations than any unit in American military history, including 9,500 Purple Hearts, 52 Distinguished Service Crosses, seven Distinguished Unit Citations, and 23 Medals of Honor (twenty-two of which were belatedly awarded by President Clinton in 2000, fifteen of them posthumously). Surely if there was American bravery on the battlefields of Europe in World War II, it was typified by the soldiers of the 442nd. Yet Roger depicts them as caricatures of Japanese *samurai*—rows of highly stylized faces behind a sword-wielding, face-painted warrior in battle pose whose clothing bears the Japanese characters for the numerals "4 4 2."

As another example, consider the piece entitled *Justified Internment* (see catalog entry #21). Howard Coble is a long-serving and therefore rather powerful member of the U.S. House of Representatives from my state of North Carolina. He is a member of the House Judiciary Committee and chairs a subcommittee on terrorism and homeland security. Back in 1988, Coble was among the Congressmen who spoke and voted against the Civil Liberties Act of 1988, which provided an apology and token redress payments to surviving internees. In February of 2003, Coble told a North Carolina radio station that he supported Franklin Roosevelt's decision to evict and detain Japanese Americans in 1942. He also offered his view that Roosevelt had made the internment decision for the benefit of Japanese Americans, to protect them from vigilante violence. His comments triggered an outcry from Japanese Americans and civil liberties groups, but Coble stood his ground. He never publicly apologized, although he did eventually concede that from the perspective of today we can see that Roosevelt's decision was wrong.

Like the image of the *samurai* of the *442nd*, Roger's image of Congressman Coble is not notable for its subtlety. In bold lines and big blocks of dull color he depicts the Congressman as an internment camp sentry in fatigues and helmet against a background of barbed wire. From his perch in a guard tower he points a rifle down toward the internment camp below him. He smiles smugly out at the viewer, as if to say, "Don't you worry about these internees. One false move and I'll blast 'em."

This approach to relating aspects of the story of the Japanese American experience in World War II is foreign to me as a lawyer. To be sure, the Japanese American internment generated a host of questions, but the ones we continue to think about and debate tend to be nuanced. There is, for example, the question of whether Korematsu v. United States, the 1944 decision in which the United States Supreme Court upheld the constitutional validity of the eviction of Japanese Americans from the West Coast, remains, as we lawyers like to say, "good law." (A case is "good law" if it states a legal principle that has never been overruled or so clearly called into question that it may no longer safely be cited as support for a legal argument.) My own view is that Korematsu is no longer good law. Eight of the nine currently sitting Supreme Court Justices have criticized the Korematsu opinion; some have even compared it to the infamous Dred Scott decision, which, in holding that slaves could not be U.S. citizens, was a factor that led to the Civil War. My view is not the only view, however. Other scholars note that the Supreme Court has never formally overruled Korematsu, and has continued to use aspects of its reasoning in other cases. The question is a close and subtle one.

Broader legal questions also linger. For example, the government's 1944 demand that Japanese Americans emerge from behind barbed wire to join the army and fight for someone else's freedom leaves us unresolved questions about whether there should be limits on what the government can demand of citizens or on how a citizen can permissibly protest government policy during wartime. The military draft was, in a basic sense, an unconscionable demand. The government had stripped the internees of every benefit of their U.S. citizenship, yet was simultaneously seeking to exact citizenship's greatest burden. Did this go too far? Did it relieve the internees of their obligations as citizens? Was resistance to the draft an acceptable means for the internees to express their disagreement with their government's policies?

Also pertinent today are lingering questions about racial profiling and national security. For sixty years we did not have to ask ourselves what the fundamental error of the Japanese American internment was, because no government policies resembled it, and we did not risk repeating the mistake. But ethnicity- and religion-conscious antiterrorism measures after September 11 have forced us to ask ourselves that question. Was the basic error of the Japanese American internment that the government made an inference about dangerousness on the unadorned basis of ethnicity? Or was the basic error instead the enormity of the deprivations that the government inflicted on the basis of that inference? If it was the former, then singling out Arabs or Muslims today for any sort of investigative inquiry, no matter how mild and non-intrusive, would seem to repeat the basic mistake of the internment. If it was the latter, then perhaps the precedent of the Japanese American internment might leave some room for non-burdensome racial, ethnic, or religious profiling.

Or consider the nightmare scenario of a "dirty" nuclear weapon detonated in an American urban center, where tens or hundreds of thousands of innocent civilians might be injured or killed. If it could be shown that an ethnicity- or religion-based internment program could prevent such a cataclysm—and that is an absurdly big "if"—then would the disastrous precedent of the Japanese American internment still place such a plan off-limits?

Finally, we continue to debate questions about the appropriate attribution of causation and responsibility for the internment program. There is near universal agreement that the decision to evict and incarcerate the West Coast's Japanese American population was the product of a basic racist and hysterical misperception of the risk to national security that Japanese Americans posed. However, hints of a Japanese effort to recruit U.S.-citizen spies in decrypted diplomatic transmissions have led some to speculate about a real national security threat. Although the overwhelming weight of evidence favors the explanation based in racism and wartime hysteria, a debate about how to interpret the decrypted diplomatic cables continues. In addition, a difficult debate lingers about the degree of moral responsibility that can fairly be attributed to the planners of the government's program of removal and detention. Many maintain that the President and his top planners deserve harsh condemnation for their decision to impose such a massive deprivation of civil liberties on an entire ethnic group. Some, however, insist that these men acted consistently with the worldview of their historical era, and therefore do not deserve blame for a wrong that is only evident in hindsight.

These are difficult questions that can—and should—trigger hours of thoughtful and careful debate.

Yet even as a law professor I confess that there is a creeping danger in this mode of close reflection and careful debate. The danger is that all of this ratiocination might dull us to the outrage of our government's placing around 120,000 people behind barbed wire in some of the most desolate regions of the United States on the simple basis of their ethnicity. It might dull us to the disruption, the dislocation, the disorientation, and the despair that this government program brought into so many innocent lives. It might dull us to the vicious, dehumanizing stereotypes that loomed so large in the minds of most white Americans in the era of the Yellow Peril.

For me as a lawyer, Roger's artwork is a jolt from another world, and a much-needed one. I look at a work like *442nd* and am forced to see the Japanese American soldier through the eyes of stereotype and prejudice. The image's viewpoint simply forces me there; I have no other choice. It is no response to a work such as this to say, "Oh, but this is an unfair exaggeration; Americans did not really see Japanese American soldiers as *samurai* warriors." That misses the point entirely. It is no doubt true that most Americans did not see members of the 442nd Regimental Combat Team as sword-wielding *samurai*. But it is also true that the

American military saw Japanese Americans as something other than true and full Americans, inappropriate for integration into units with white soldiers. I am reminded of the words that a white military officer spoke at the Minidoka Relocation Center (where Roger spent a few years of his childhood) in welcoming new Japanese American draftees into the Army. "We in the American armed forces," he said to the crowd of U.S. citizens, "are happy to welcome you Japanese among our ranks, even though your country, Japan, is at war with the United States." Roger's image *442* captures the outrage in that statement in ways that reasoned delineation and debate cannot.

In the same way, Roger's casting of U.S. Congressman Howard Coble as a weapon-toting internment camp guard in *Justified Internment* is surely, in some basic way, unfair. Yet a debate about whether this image is or is not fair to the congressman—like the debate about the fairness of condemning Franklin Roosevelt and his advisers—subtly shifts our attention to the rights and entitlements of those who designed this massive civil rights violation, and those who continue to defend it. The audacity of Roger's characterization of Coble forcibly grabs our viewpoint and places it in the eyes of those victimized sixty years ago by the government's program, and now re-victimized by a powerful official's defense of it.

As we think and debate our way through the enormously difficult legal and moral issues that the September 11 attacks bequeathed us, we need to do more than think and debate. We also need to feel. Roger's stunning, jolting work helps us in this enterprise in ways that no legal analysis could possibly replace.

"That's for Your Ayatollah, You Chinaman!"
Art, Ethics, and Social Injustice

Daniel Wueste

I should begin with an explanation of the title of this piece. The quotation is taken from the descriptive statement that accompanies *Iran Hostage Crisis*, a work from Roger Shimomura's *Stereotypes* and *Admonitions* series, which is also included in this exhibition (see catalog entry #20). The triad of concepts in the second part of the title was much on my mind as I thought about that image and the admonition that accompanies it. It is now a fixture of my thinking about the work of Roger Shimomura; it is also the focus of this essay.

The event that this image represents took place in 1987 during the Hostage Crisis in Iran. That was eighteen years ago, but the sad social fact vividly represented in the work is as fresh and real as the bagel I had for breakfast today. The prompts for such visceral and vicious racism change. In 1987 it was hostages in Iran, in 1941 it was the attack on Pearl Harbor; today, that is in 2005, the driver flipping his middle finger at an Asian American would probably say something like, "that's for all your towel head buddies, you Chinaman!" and the event would be explained by reference to the attacks of September 11, 2001.

The observation that for the American public, the enemy today is similar to earlier enemies is certainly apt: His religion is foreign and his fanatical devotion to it is suicidal. He is secretive, sinister, barbaric. And, perhaps most important, if only because it is the easiest characteristic to see, the enemy is not white. The warning that we've been there before and must take care not to go there again is well taken.[1] It is difficult, however, to be sanguine about the likelihood that the warning will be heeded. It's too easy for Americans, not known for their historical acuity in any case, to forget the past, particularly if it is unhappy or ugly. If not forgotten, it is all too often conveniently repackaged—it won't do to have something ugly

1. See Eric Muller, "An Arab American Internment?" http://www.press.uchicago.edu/News/911muller.html, first published in *Pacific Citizen*. Evidence that there is real danger here and that there is something quite unhealthy in the air is very easy to find on the Internet. See, for example, "Terrorism is NOT equal to ISLAM or 'Towel Heads'" http://dotfaf.com/archives/print_000302.php, especially the comments in reply, and "JACL Condemns Outrageous and Indefensible Tsunami Song," http://www.jacl.org/current_prs/JACL%20Condemns%20Outrageous%20and%20Indefensible%20Tsunami%20Song.pdf (these sites accessed June 30, 2005).

2. "N.C. Rep.: WWII Internment Camps Were Meant to Help," Associated Press, Wednesday, February 05, 2003 http://www.foxnews.com/story/0,2933,77677,00.html (accessed July 4, 2005). "Coble, who lives in Greensboro, said Japanese-Americans were 'an endangered species' during World War II and needed to be put into internment camps for their own protection." Rob Christensen, "Ethnic gaffes: a triple play," (Raleigh) News & Observer http://www.newsobserver.com/politics/christensen/2003/story/1257458p-7369915c.html (accessed July 4, 2005).

3. Quoted in William Lew, "Return of the Yellow Peril: The Works of Roger Shimomura," Catalogue for the exhibition at Cheney Cowles Museum, Spokane, Washington.

4. Idem.

5. Roger Shimomura, "The 63 Stages of the Yellow Brick Road," Keynote at the CAA Annual Conference, February 19, 2003, CAA News http://www.collegeart.org/caa/news/2003/May/RogerShimomura.html (accessed June 24, 2005).

on the shelf—or brushed aside; as if awareness of history's lessons were a matter of fashion—vogue today, passé tomorrow—or mere political correctness, rather than something that needs to be sustained. It is so much nicer, for example, to think of the internment of Japanese Americans in the way suggested by U.S. Representative Howard Coble, as largely paternalistic: "We were at war. They (Japanese-Americans) were an endangered species," Coble said. "For many of these Japanese-Americans, it wasn't safe for them to be on the street."[2] Shimomura's *Justified Internment* undermines Coble's paternalism claim in a straightforward and powerful way (see catalog entry #21). It makes forgetting or repackaging more difficult. That is a noteworthy aspect of the painting that contributes heartily to its value as a work of art.

As I read about Roger Shimomura and familiarized myself with his work, what I found most striking is the moral thrust and commitment in his art. However, I learned from William Lew that the activist strain that I perceived wasn't always present (or acknowledged). For instance, Lew points to an interview from 1975 in which Shimomura remarks, "The subject isn't important; the manipulation is…I don't want anything to interfere with the visual concept. I'm interested in pure design." In 1981, speaking of work in his *Diary* series, Shimomura indicates that the diaries were "an excuse to do a painting" (see catalog entries #4 and #5). He goes on to say that he's not really interested "in moving anyone about the situation my grandmother was in." The paintings, he says, aren't political: "They're not my protest. My protest is donating money and time toward Japanese Americans seeking reparations." It's okay if the "paintings bring the issue up," but, apparently, at this juncture that was not his aim.[3] What of the *Minidoka* series? Lew reports that the series was born of Shimomura's experience viewing a slide presentation by an elderly Japanese American who had been incarcerated at Minidoka. This slide presentation "so jarred him that he saw the necessity to render his response to the camp experience in painting."[4] Lew's report resonates with Shimomura's reply to a reporter's question whether he could summarize his most important message to his students over the years. His reply was, "I tell my students to 'take a hard look at yourself first and consider whether there is significant value in sharing what you are experiencing in life.'"[5] This is a major shift, from talk of "an excuse for a painting" to talk of the value for others in sharing one's life experience. We start with an artistic posture for which meaning and purpose, if we use those terms at all, will be congeneric ("the manipulation," "pure design"), and move to one where the meaning and purpose of art is consciously extrageneric (vividly representing and decrying racism and injustice, for example).[6]

The breadth and the value of the artistic enterprise are much greater here. From this vantage point art can be a means to an end beyond itself; it can engage with things beyond its own boundaries. Thus, while with the earlier posture it is difficult to see how art is properly subject to *moral* evaluation, let alone how it makes sense to talk about the moral responsibility of artists, after the shift has occurred, what was at best very puzzling is now fairly easy to see and understand. For now it will be granted readily that art can tease, titillate, taunt, and teach; that it can touch us deeply and take us to places we have never been before; that it is potentially an instrument of social transformation and moral growth.

For many of us, I suspect, this point about the breadth and value of the arts is a commonplace. Indeed, those who think first of theatre or literature may regard it as something approaching a self-evident truth. But those steeped in art or music criticism, particularly those who are familiar with the work of Clement Greenberg or Eduard Hanslick respectively, will recognize the distinction between the two postures identified above and the pull of the former for those who prefer "pure," "fine," or "high" art. I certainly recall the look of dismay and concern on my professor's face when, in an aesthetics course, I suggested that music often conveys nonmusical (extrageneric) meaning. His response was to announce that I must not have read the assignment (Hanslick) carefully. I replied that I had read it with care and that Hanslick's theoretical position simply did not comport well with the reality I knew firsthand as a musician. Unfortunately for me, when I responded to his query about the venues I played (clubs and colleges), I was told that my experience did not count. I was the stereotypical amateur with an ax; "Hanslick was not talking about that kind of music, if that is in fact music. Well, let's move on..." The anecdote will have more punch if we pause to consider the view that was being foisted upon me as plainly correct after my suggestion was summarily dismissed.

Greenberg is quite clear. "The fact is, that art of any kind, literature included, doesn't operate as a moral or any other kind of agent. It operates only for itself and only for what we can get from that self in abstraction, as it were, from whatever else....When it does that, art is morally, politically, and socially indifferent." As Greenberg has it, if one's aim is to make sense of art, the chances of success are greatest if one approaches it "as autonomous, as being abstracted from all political, social, economic, or religious or moral issues or factors." He goes further: "I repeat: asking art to serve a moral, or any other end except aesthetic quality, is to make an illegitimate demand on art."[7]

Critics and theoreticians have put much ink to paper exploring the cases for and against such a view. It is not my purpose here, however, to enter the debate on one side or the other.

6. I take the terms 'congeneric' and 'extrageneric' from Leonard Meyer. Meyer, *Emotion and Meaning in Music* (Chicago: University of Chicago Press, 1956). Congeneric meaning stays within the boundaries of an artistic medium. Extrageneric meaning, on the other hand, is not constrained in this way. In *The Beautiful in Music* (1854) Eduard Hanslick famously insisted that all meaning in music is what Meyer calls congeneric meaning. It does not (and cannot) go beyond the boundaries of the medium, sound: "Music has no subject beyond the combinations of notes we hear, for music speaks not only by means of sounds, it speaks nothing but sound." Wolfgang Sandberger, liner notes (1996). *Intimate Letters*. Sony Classical SK 66840. Translated by Stewart Spencer.

7. Clement Greenberg, "Autonomies of Art," Moral Philosophy and Art Symposium, Mountain Lake, Virginia, October 1980, online: http://www.sharecom.ca/greenberg/autonomies.html (accessed July 4, 2005). Greenberg is not alone in making the strong claim of illegitimacy. See for example, Donald Kuspit, "Art and the Moral Imperative: Analyzing Activist Art," *New Art Examiner* 18.5 (1991)18-25. Kuspit argues that using art for a moral purpose is both "fundamentally inappropriate," and, in the end, "inherently anti-art."

8. See for example, Kuspit, "Art and the Moral Imperative," who inveighs against artists who do this. He calls them "moralizing artists."

9. A complete response to this view is beyond the scope of this article and this endnote.However, this much can be said. There is nothing "anti art" in allowing the artistic enterprise to expand in the direction of social justice. Indeed, most would count this as moral growth. Artists, no less than other professionals, should be encouraged to use the resources they have to address and counter social injustice. A theory that disallows this is altogether too cramped. To be sure, artistic responses to social injustice are not obligatory, but they certainly are permissible both morally and in light of the normative constraints implicit in the artistic enterprise.

10. Clement Greenberg, "Autonomies of Art."

11. Shimomura, "The 63 Stages of the Yellow Brick Road."

There are several reasons for this, but two stand out. First, it is not clear that the debaters are correct in their assumption that there are only two choices (the Greenbergian position sketched above and its denial). Second, the sense in which it is "illegitimate" to ask art to serve an extrageneric purpose is elusive. Is it that art cannot be used in this way or is it that it *should* not be used this way? Since it is clear that art can be used in this way,[8] it must be the latter. In that case, however, one is likely to be embarrassed by the answer to the obvious question, namely, what is the sense of 'should' here. If it has a moral sense, talk of illegitimacy in moral applications of art (generally rather than specifically) smacks of paradox. If it is essentially or purely aesthetic, we confront the challenge of explaining, in a non-question begging way, what talk of aesthetic illegitimacy comes to.

If one assesses the shift we have been discussing from the Greenbergian posture, one sense in which it is significant should be clear. One has opened the door to questions about the legitimacy of one's work, perhaps even charges of "treason" in the sense of now being engaged in activities that are at bottom anti-art.[9] Another significant upshot of the shift is that it entails a basic change in the way one's work is measured. Shimomura speaks to this directly indicating first that his decision to link his art to his ethnic identity "was not a career decision." He writes, "Customarily, some art-world power brokers are attempting to decide, for a few of us, what we have been doing, why we have been doing it, and, now, why it is time to move on." However, in his own case, as perhaps in others, he says, the direction of the work emerges from "circumstances and the imperative response," rather than "art trend [or] academic training." As if responding to the Greenbergian prescription that an artist should "transcend or abstract himself from every historical circumstance except that of art itself,"[10] Shimomura continues,

> Art about the cultural politics of difference cannot be measured by the same formula as Impressionism, Abstract Expressionism, and Color Field painting. Social injustices and racial prejudice continue to be in season. Unfortunately, some critics do not make any distinction between what is reality for some people and what is fashionably smart for others.[11]

You will recall William Lew's report about the genesis of the *Minidoka* series. It emerged from circumstances (viewing of a slide show, among other things) and the series of paintings was Shimomura's imperative response. This link between life experiences and art as imperative response, and in particular, the way it is manifest in Shimomura's work and forcefully engages the viewer, explains the three ideas in my title—art, ethics, and social injustice. In what follows I will focus on this triad of concepts.

In 1963, in his "Letter from a Birmingham Jail," Martin Luther King said, "Injustice anywhere is a threat to justice everywhere." One obvious implication of this observation is that injustice ought not be ignored. If we inquire why, we can state King's answer quickly: it is dangerous to do so; the consequences of a failure to respond are likely to include the spread of injustice. Our question might be answered in other ways as well. For example, it might be said that failure to respond is unfair to those who suffer injustice; that reflection reveals that neither you nor I would agree to a rule that allowed others to ignore the injustice you or I were suffering simply because, for example, it was inconvenient to respond. Or again, one might say, look, failing to respond to injustice is not the sort of thing that makes it easy for me to look at myself in the mirror in the morning; this is not the sort of thing that gets me closer to what I aspire to be—a person of admirable character. And, of course, the last point might be made from the perspective of a community or a nation. These responses exhibit three ethical frameworks, that is, three approaches for figuring out what ought, morally, to be done. The first speaks in terms of consequences; the second speaks in terms of deserved treatment (fairness) and rejects special pleading in favor of rules that apply equally to all; the third speaks in terms of aspirations to excellence, to what we aspire to be as individuals or a nation. There is, then, an ethical imperative to respond to injustice. And, significantly, we can meet the challenge to justify the claim that such an imperative exists by pointing to the considerations adumbrated above. Moreover, we might note that what we have here is a converging set of ethical considerations; our confidence in this judgment is the upshot of that convergence. [12]

The incarceration by the government of the United States of 120,000 persons of Japanese ancestry living in the United States during World War II was a grave injustice. Roger Shimomura's imperative response to it, the *Minidoka* series, answers to the ethical imperative in Dr. King's observation. If these paintings do not make it impossible to forget or ignore that injustice, they at least make it difficult for any sensitive viewer to do so. In this respect, these paintings are quite like the moral rules we learn as we mature; neither can guarantee the outcome they aim at. Shimomura's moral/political response to the injustice of the internment did not begin nor does it end with these paintings. As you will recall, before he made the move from the first to the second of the two artistic postures discussed above, he was already contributing time and money to the cause of reparations for the internees. His paintings are,

12. See "A Philosophical Yet User-friendly Framework For Ethical Decision Making in Critical Care Nursing," *Dimensions of Critical Care Nursing* 24 (2) (March/April 2005): 70-79. The article is best accessed online (e.g., through a library e-journals access system). The printed version includes multiple editorial mistakes; they have been corrected by the publisher in the online version.

13. Shimomura, "The 63 Stages of the Yellow Brick Road." Alice Walker is the author of several highly acclaimed novels, the best known, perhaps, is *The Color Purple*. See, for example, http://www.gale-group.com/free_resources/bhm/bio/walker_a.htm (accessed July 5, 2005).

then, an element of his response to this injustice. In light of their reach (the number of people touched by them) and power, they constitute a substantial contribution to the cause.

Injustice comes in many forms. Unjust imprisonment is clearly one of them; indeed, it is paradigmatic. One may be imprisoned behind bars or, as in the case of the Japanese American internees, behind a fence of barbed wire. Still another way in which a person may be imprisoned, in the sense of having one's liberty effectively constrained, is the result of the way they are seen by others. Shimomura attributes his recognition of the fact that stereotypes are prisons of this sort to writer Alice Walker.[13] The truly pernicious stereotypes of Asians that Shimomura presents so vividly in his work direct our moral attention to another serious injustice that ought not be ignored. The injustice of the stereotypes is not simply that in America certain opportunities are denied to Asians, it's that this denial of liberty is based on *morally irrelevant* factors such as ancestry, skin color, or physical appearance. Suppose blue-eyed blondes were refused seating at Dennys, ejected from the restaurant by security personnel, and then beaten by a mob as the security people stood by, *because* they were blue-eyed blondes. The injustice here is patent; it is no less patent in the scenario presented to us in Shimomura's *Dennys Incident* (see catalog entry #13), though as the narrative that accompanies the painting notes, the physical harm that was inflicted on four of the Asian American students notwithstanding, the wrong in this case was not recognized (officially!). Injustice of this sort is addressed in many of Shimomura's paintings, for example, *The Gook, Housing Discrimination, Do You Speak English, Not an Indian (variation #2), The History of Art*. This last example, like two others in the exhibition, *Florence South Carolina*, and *Back to the West Coast*, make the key point forcefully, namely, that the situations the images take us into are governed by how Shimomura is seen by others. For instance, in the real situations associated with *The History of Art* (see catalog entry #18) and *Florence South Carolina* (see catalog entry #15), Shimomura might as well have been dressed as he is in the paintings; his otherness in the minds of the others is that striking; for them it is impossible to ignore. Sadly, what they cannot get past is utterly, completely, and morally irrelevant to the matter at hand, hence the injustice.

A key feature of stereotypes is that they do not reflect reality; they *create* a reality. The reality thus created consists in this alone: they are in fact operative in the world irrationally dictating responses that vary in their viciousness but are alike in this: they perpetrate injustice. As Glen Brown observes, "stereotypes—as Shimomura's works so forcefully attest—originate and are sustained exclusively within representation."[14] He goes on, rightly in my view, to suggest that representation is, then, the best way to combat them.

The injustice created by stereotypes, which is rightly cast as a form of unjust imprisonment, is best answered in the medium of representation, which is where Roger Shimomura has chosen to contribute to the cause of overcoming it. It cannot seriously be denied that such injustice is real; nor that the attacks of September 11, 2001, have exacerbated the problem. Consequently, there is work to be done, for as noted earlier, injustice ought not be ignored. If the points above are well taken, artists are especially well positioned to undertake this work. It may even be morally incumbent on them to do so, if we agree with Lucy Lippard that artists "have not yet earned the luxury of poeticizing rather than politicizing [their] work."[15] Of course, in responding to injustice of this sort one has to have a realistic expectation about the likelihood of success. It's not as if the ignorance, boorishness, and insensitivity that underlie racism and prejudice can be overcome (defeated) by one person or by a single means. After all, they did not arise from a single source—their origins are complex and sad. The task is large. Those who undertake it, such as Roger Shimomura, are doing important work, not least because they are showing us that and how art can respond to the ethical imperative to counter social injustice.

14. Glen Brown, "Identity and Erasure," *Asian Art News*, March/April 2002, p. 53.

15. Quoted in Shimomura, "The 63 Stages of the Yellow Brick Road."

Midwife at Minidoka:
Toku Shimomura and World War II

Susan L. Smith

1. For a fuller discussion of the history of Toku Shimomura and other *Issei* women, see Susan L. Smith, *Japanese American Midwives: Culture, Community, and Health Politics, 1880-1950* (Urbana: University of Illinois Press, 2005). I would like to acknowledge the vital support and valuable insights of the members of my writing group at the University of Alberta: Lesley Cormack, Judith Garber, Susan Hamilton, Lois Harder, Daphne Read, and Teresa Zackodnik.

Many of Roger Shimomura's paintings of the incarceration of his family and other Japanese Americans during World War II were inspired by the diaries of his grandmother, Toku Shimomura (1888-1968). As an artist and grandson, Roger found images of family pride and political injustice within Toku's diary entries written in Idaho at the Minidoka Relocation Center, one of ten camps run by the federal government during the war. Who was the woman in the paintings?

Toku's diaries have not only inspired Roger's art, they are also a rich resource for historians.[1] Her diaries are important for the study of women's history because there is so little primary material available that tells the story of World War II from the perspective of Japanese American women, especially women of the immigrant generation. They help us understand the experience of being in the camps even when few of those who lived through incarceration are still alive. They provide information about how war affected the lives of individuals and how people found ways to cope. By presenting information about a specific woman's experiences, Toku's diaries humanize a tragic moment in American history (see catalog entries #2 and #4).

Toku's diaries demonstrate that she made important contributions to wartime community survival through her informal caregiving labor. Toku's diaries are a necessary corrective to what other sources, especially official government records, suggest about women and the wartime incarceration. In official records, *Issei* (Japanese immigrant) women appear as marginal, insignificant figures. Yet, Toku's diary provides evidence of an *Issei* woman at work. Although some *Issei* women, especially those engaged in farm work, hoped that camp life would give them a break from endless agricultural labor, most women did not stop working in camp. Toku, like many *Issei* women, did not have a paid job in camp, but she still performed household labor and contributed to camp life by addressing the needs of a population living in confinement. Despite the frustrations and fears engendered by the forced evacuation of the West Coast Japanese Americans, Toku and other *Issei* women continued to labor for their families and friends, and support each other. Toku was not only the wife, mother, and grandmother of Roger Shimomura's paintings; she was also a working woman—a midwife and a community caregiver.

THE DIARY OF TOKU SHIMOMURA

Toku kept a diary for fifty-six years and, despite the wartime upheaval, her family had the foresight to save it. Day after day Toku wrote in a conventional printed diary or *nikki*, a habit of a growing number of middle-class, urban women in Japan in the early twentieth century.[2] Toku, however, wrote her diary in the United States—it is an American diary written in Japanese. She began it aboard the ship Awa Maru on which she travelled to America in 1912, at a time when thousands of Japanese women immigrated to Hawai'i and the North American mainland. She wrote in her diary almost daily until 1968, the year she died.

It appears that Toku wrote in her diaries only for herself. Her approach was in contrast to the early Japanese diary tradition, which assumed an audience, usually of family members who were to gain instruction and inspiration from reading the diary. Toku, apparently, had no intention of having others read it. Yet she also showed little concern about protecting the privacy of her writings. She made no provision to have the diary destroyed upon her death, or to pass it on to her children, or to have it published. She simply left the volumes of her diary in the care of her husband.[3]

As an organized and efficient person, Toku kept a diary as part of ordering her life. There is often little in it about her interior life, especially before World War II. In general, she rarely used her diary as "an expression of the self" or to process her feelings, especially during the late 1910s and 1920s when she was raising young children and busy with her midwifery practice. This relative absence of emotional display was typical of the diary writings of Japanese women of the nineteenth and early twentieth centuries, even if it is surprising and disappointing to the modern reader.[4]

2. Nishikawa Yūko, "Diaries as Gendered Texts," in *Women and Class in Japanese History*, eds. Hitomi Tonomura, Anne Walthall, and Wakita Haruko (Ann Arbor: Center for Japanese Studies, University of Michigan, 1999): 241-55, especially 243.

3. Nishikawa, "Diaries as Gendered Texts," 244-45, 250; Roger Shimomura, interview by author, tape recording, Lawrence, Kansas, 16 June 1998.

4. Nishikawa, "Diaries as Gendered Texts," 244.

5. For information on Toku Shimomura's early life, see Ito Kazu, *Zoku Hokubei Hyakunen-Zakura: Volume 2* (Seattle: Hokubei Hyakunen-zakura Jikko Iinkai, 1968), English translation courtesy of Roger Shimomura. The entries for January to March 1912 have been commented on and reprinted in Kazuo Ito, *Issei: A History of Japanese Immigrants in North America*, translated by Shinichiro Nakamura and Jean S. Gerard (Seattle: Japanese Community Service, 1973), 8-11. See also Register of the State Medical Examination Board, State of Washington, 1917, Licensing Department, Washington State Archives. Brief excerpts of Toku's diary can be found in Donald Keene, *Modern Japanese Diaries: The Japanese at Home and Abroad as Revealed Through Their Diaries* (Henry Holt and Co., 1995), 321-26, and in Franklin Odo, ed., *The Columbia Documentary History of the Asian American Experience* (N.Y.: Columbia University Press, 2002), 274-80.

Although the diary was not usually an emotional record, it does reveal something of her relationships to others and the mutual benefits of the emotional sustenance the relationships provided. Toku not only wrote of the weather, but also of her various activities and social contacts, including housekeeping, social engagements, her health, and the health of family members, friends, and clients. She wrote down the names of people she saw and unusual or interesting events in her day. At times the diary seems to be merely the place in which she kept track of her incredibly busy social life. Yet, it is a record of the daily life of an American *sanba* or midwife. Japanese American midwives were women who established their expertise as childbirth attendants in Japan, but spent most of their working lives in the United States. The diary entries are her personal and professional archive. The entries, however brief, illuminate the contours of her life, one shaped by connections to others.

The diary reveals little about Toku Shimomura before she came to Seattle, Washington. We know that she was born Toku Machida on 12 June 1888, in Saitama Prefecture in central Japan near Tokyo. She was the eldest daughter of a forester. She trained as a nurse and midwife at the Japanese Red Cross Hospital and Nursing School in Tokyo, graduating in 1905 at the age of seventeen. In the midst of the Russo-Japanese war of 1904-1905, she worked as a Red Cross nurse and helped treat the wounded on a hospital ship of the Japanese Imperial Navy. After the war she worked in a hospital as a nurse and/or midwife at the Ishikawa Silk Mill in the city of Kamagoe.[5]

A PICTURE BRIDE ARRIVES IN SEATTLE

In 1912, Toku sailed to Seattle to meet her husband-to-be, Yoshitomi Shimomura. She was one of the thousands of picture brides who came to the United States in the early twentieth century. Picture brides were the wives from newly arranged marriages between Japanese men living in the United States and women in Japan. The picture bride practice was, in many ways, merely an extension of the tradition of arranged marriages in Japan, only now through an exchange of photographs. At twenty-three years old, Toku felt unprepared and a bit afraid when she left Japan with sixty other pictures brides and her future brother-in-law, the hospital superintendent from the silk mill where she had worked. Before departing for Seattle, where Toku would meet her new husband, she visited his parents. They treated her very kindly and, as she recalled in her diary, "My heart leaped as I stood in front of the picture of my future husband."[6] Before her departure she also stopped to check on one of her pregnant clients, indicating that she had already begun practicing midwifery in Japan, possibly at the silk mill. She noted in her diary that she was very sad to leave her family and friends, and that she expected to stay in the United States for about ten years. Some thirty people came to the train station to bid her farewell. As a member of several women's organizations she had developed a large circle of friends, many of whom she continued to correspond with over the years. Leaving was very hard and she wrote, "I have cried so much lately I should soon run out of tears."[7]

Toku believed that she was more educated and cultured than her husband and she was probably right. There is evidence that the average educational level of *Issei* women was equal to or sometimes higher than that of *Issei* men. Scholars note that many Japanese immigrant women had studied at American mission schools in Japan. Other women may have agreed to immigrate because they were older, seen as less attractive, or divorced. Such women were more readily available as picture brides, even if it meant marrying below their class, because they were seen as less marriageable in Japan.[8]

Toku had several reasons to marry Yoshitomi. One reason was the encouragement of the hospital superintendent at the Ishikawa Silk Mill, who wanted to see his brother-in-law make a good match. Yoshitomi was the brother of the superintendent's wife. Toku also married on the basis of information that Yoshitomi had graduated from business school and shared her Christian faith.[9] Toku became a Christian in Japan and she was one of the early members of the Seattle Japanese Methodist Church, established in 1904. Methodist churches actively recruited Japanese immigrants throughout the West Coast, and like other Christian missions, provided people with information about employment and lodging, and care when they were sick. Toku remained very active in the church throughout her life.[10]

AN AMERICAN *SANBA*

Above all, Toku's life in Seattle was shaped by her work as a midwife. Yet, outside of the family members of Japanese immigrant midwives, the significance of midwifery to Japanese immigrant communities remained unknown to later generations. Midwifery was not a part of the health culture of the American-born *Nisei* and *Sansei*, so Japanese American midwives have not registered as important historical figures within Japanese American

6. Toku Shimomura's diary, 12 January 1912. Access to the original volumes of Toku Shimomura's diary was courtesy of Roger Shimomura of Lawrence, Kansas. I am deeply indebted to Roger for allowing me to examine these treasured diaries. I also thank Febe Pamonag, Valerie Hentiuk, and Teko Gardener of Edmonton and Ms. Okano, employed by the Japan Foundation at the Kansai Language Institute in Osaka, Japan, for their translation assistance.

7. Toku Shimomura's diary, 21 February 1912.

8. Toku Shimomura's diary, January to March 1912; Interview with Roger Shimomura; Eileen Sunada Sarasohn, *Issei Women: Echoes From Another Frontier* (Palo Alto, California: Pacific Books, 1998), 70, 146.

9. Excerpts of Toku Shimomura's 1912 diary in Ito, *Zoku Hokubei Hyakunen-Zakura*, English translation.

10. Interview with Roger Shimomura; S. Frank Miyamoto, "An Immigrant Community in America," in *East Across the Pacific: Historical and Sociological Studies of Japanese Immigration and Assimilation*, ed. by Hilary Conroy and T. Scott Miyakawa (Santa Barbara, Calif.: Clio Press, 1972), 232-4; Ito, *Issei*, 274, 908; Linda Tamura, *The Hood River Issei: An Oral History of Japanese Settlers in Oregon's Hood River Valley* (Urbana: University of Illinois Press, 1993), 51, 126-29.

11. Toku Shimomura, quoted in Ito, *Issei*, 860.

12. Toku Shimomura's diary, August and October 1913, 1922-1923, 1926; Toku quoted in Kazuo Ito, *Issei*, 250, 859.

communities or scholarly literature. Yet, midwives delivered most of the babies of the immigrant generation in Hawai'i and the American West.

Toku was one of the busiest Japanese midwives or *sanba* in Seattle and able to earn a steady income. "I delivered nearly a thousand babies in twenty-seven years," she wrote in later years.[11] Toku received her midwife license in Washington in 1917 at the age of twenty-nine. According to Toku, midwife licensing facilitated the midwives' efforts to set a standard fee. Before 1917 she stated that they charged about $15 per birth, but after receiving the new state license they charged about $35. Payment to midwives covered many hours of health care service, including prenatal and postnatal care visits and staying overnight during a delivery.[12] A midwife earned a good income compared to many wage earners, but still less than a doctor. Toku's diaries record that she delivered fifty births per year in the early 1920s, at the height of the *Issei* baby boom in Seattle. In the 1930s, Toku and most *Issei* midwives stopped delivering babies regularly as the *Nisei* began to have their children. By 1940, just before the war with Japan began, the entries in Toku's diary show that she had retired from midwifery. Yet, it remained an important component of Toku's identity.

WORLD WAR II

World War II brought dramatic changes to the lives of Japanese Americans, including Toku Shimomura. Beginning in 1942, Toku's diary entries illustrate the hardships she and others faced during their removal from their homes to one of sixteen West Coast assembly centers, including Puyallup, and then one of ten inland camps, including Minidoka. The prison-like camps, popularly referred to as "internment camps," were run by the War Relocation Authority (WRA), a newly established civilian agency of the federal government.

The forced relocation created a situation in which a health care system had to be built from scratch to care for a vast population placed in camps in desolate locations. Inside each WRA camp, which held from about 8,000 to nearly 20,000 people, the government constructed and staffed a hospital. Officials represented such health care resources as a sign of government concern for the welfare of those incarcerated and an indication that they were treated humanely. Yet, despite the existence of formal medical care, the government still provided it in a physical and political environment that contributed to poor health.

Toku's diaries are important because they reveal that the care provided within the formal health care system in the assembly centers and WRA camps was not the only caregiving available. Government records are useful sources for understanding the formal health care system, but they are limited in what they can reveal about informal caregiving. However, Toku Shimomura's diary provides evidence of her participation in such caregiving. Informal caregiving includes a wide range of activities that contributed to the health and welfare of people. One cannot understand the full scope of community health care, including the emotional and psychological dimensions of health and well being, without investigating informal activity. Informal care was especially important because Japanese traditions promoted the role of family members in caring for the sick, even in hospitals.[13] Informal care, whether it is labeled home care, domestic care, family care, or community care, has been mostly women's work.[14]

Toku's diaries reveal something of what caregiving looked like outside the formal health care system. She provided a range of informal care to friends and family during the war, in the assembly center and in the WRA camp. Toku consistently made house calls or visits to the hospital because her health work, which was no longer performed for a fee, was still meaningful and important to her and to others.

PUYALLUP ASSEMBLY CENTER

At Puyallup Assembly Center, Toku's diary entries provide evidence of her attempts to address the needs of Japanese Americans living under difficult wartime conditions. In April 1942 Toku and her family, along with other Japanese American residents from Seattle, had to leave their homes and go to Puyallup, on the state fairgrounds south of Seattle. Here some 8,000 people lived as captives.[15]

Toku's diaries indicate that she made numerous house calls to visit the sick, especially other *Issei* women.[16] In July 1942 she wrote, "Between the rain showers in the afternoon, I made inquiries on the sick people in section 1 and 2. Mrs. Takiguchi's condition has become much better and we rejoiced." Later that month she indicated that "I heard Masako Nomura was not feeling well so I visited her and gave her an enema."[17] Two days later she wrote: "Setsuko Tanagi entered the hospital and I visited her. It was so hot in the rooms! It reminded me of the bathing rooms. It was more than the patients could bear." She visited Setsuko at the hospital again later that week and wrote, "I was happy to hear that her condition was progressing favorably."[18] At one point her three-year-old grandson Roger became sick,

13. Michelle Gutierrez, "Medicine in a Crisis Situation: The Effect of Culture on Health Care in the World War II Japanese American Detention Camps" (Master's thesis, California State University, Fullerton, 1989), 128; Leon H. Bruno, *The Private Japanese Hospital: A Unique Social Phenomenon on Hawaii, 1907-1960* (Hilo, Hawai'i: Lyman House Memorial Museum, 1985), 3.

14. Emily K. Abel, "Family Caregiving in the Nineteenth Century: Emily Hawley Gillespie and Sarah Gillespie, 1858-1888," *Bulletin of the History of Medicine*, 68, n. 4 (1994): 574, 576, 596-98; Peregrine Horden, "Household Care and Informal Networks: Comparisons and Continuities from Antiquity to the Present," in The *Locus of Care: Families, Communities, Institutions, and the Provision of Welfare Since Antiquity*, ed. by Peregrine Horden and Richard Smith (London and N.Y.: Routledge, 1998), 31, 39; Carol Baines, Patricia Evans, Sheila Neysmith, eds., *Women's Caring: Feminist Perspectives on Social Welfare* (Toronto: McClelland & Stewart, 1991), 28.

15. Toku Shimomura's diary, 28 April 1942, 11 May 1942, 16 May 1942, 16 September 1942; Monica Sone, *Nisei Daughter* (Seattle: University of Washington Press, 1953), 173, 177, 179.

16. For the story of health care in assembly centers, see Louis Fiset, "Public Health in World War II Assembly Centers for Japanese Americans," *Bulletin of the History of Medicine*, v. 73 (1999): 565-84.

17. Toku Shimomura's diary, 16 July, 22 July, and 24 July 1942.

18. Toku Shimomura's diary, 26 July and 29 July 1942.

19. Toku Shimomura's diary, 13 June, 14 June, 16 June, and 24 June 1942.

20. Toku Shimomura's diary, 12 July, 13 July, and 1 August 1942.

21. Toku Shimomura's diary, 1 August 1942.

22. Toku Shimomura's diary, 10 August 1942.

23. War Relocation Authority, *First Quarterly Report, March 18 to June 30, 1942* (Washington, D.C., Government Printing Office, 1942), 30; Velma B. Kessel, *Behind Barbed Wire: Heart Mountain Relocation Camp* (Powell, Wyoming: privately published, 1992); Roger Daniels, *Concentration Camps USA: Japanese Americans and World War II* (N.Y.: Holt, Rinehart and Winston, 1971), 89; Valerie Matsumoto, "Japanese American Women During World War II," in *Unequal Sisters: A Multicultural Reader in U.S. Women's History*, ed. Ellen Carol Du Bois and Vicki L. Ruiz (N.Y.: Routledge, 1990), 377.

possibly with the chicken pox, and he was put into an isolation ward in the hospital for one week. When she visited him there, she found the ward to be nothing but a "miserable" jail. It was "truly pitiful," she remarked.[19]

Toku's diary also offers evidence that she was still a midwife at heart. Her interest in maternal and infant care had not disappeared. For instance, she kept track of when babies were born in the hospital at Puyallup, noting each birth in her diary.[20] On 1 August 1942, she even went to the hospital to check on a birthing woman. "I heard that Sally Ida was having a difficult delivery. We were all very worried but she delivered a boy and we were all pleased."[21] It is not surprising that she never once suggested that these women would have been better off with a midwife-attended home birth. Horse stalls and wooden shacks, the housing provided in the assembly centers and WRA camps, were not appropriate shelters for anyone, let alone women giving birth. Although midwives like Toku were only rarely used as childbirth attendants among Japanese Americans by the time the war began, their contributions to health promotion did not cease.

MINIDOKA RELOCATION CENTER

Several months after entering the Puyallup Assembly Center, Toku and the other detainees were forced to relocate once more, this time from Washington state to Idaho. "Once again we have to move as exiles," recorded Toku.[22] In August 1942, the military moved Toku and thousands of people to Minidoka Relocation Center in the sun-baked terrain of southern Idaho.

The forced relocation of 120,000 people to remote locations, including swampland and deserts, produced a potential health care crisis of enormous proportions that was averted only because of the efforts of Japanese Americans themselves. To prevent a public health disaster, the government relied upon the expertise of *Issei* and American-born *Nisei* physicians, surgeons, dentists, optometrists, pharmacists, nurses, and nurses' aides and then paid them the extraordinarily low wage of less than $20 a month, at a time when a white nurse working in camp earned $150 a month.[23]

The government did not, however, turn to *Issei* women like Toku Shimomura to address health needs in camp. According to evidence from several WRA camps, there simply was no place for the practice of midwifery in the health care system.[24] Instead, health policy mandated that all births take place in camp hospitals.

Health care was a central issue in the WRA camps. Like the sites of the assembly centers, the environment and housing facilities of the WRA camps were not conducive to healthy living. Furthermore, Idaho was a big shock for Seattle residents who were used to a mild, rainy climate. In the Minidoka camp, dust storms reigned and temperatures regularly exceeded 100°F (see catalog entry #5). [25]

Toku, and no doubt other *Issei* women health workers, continued to provide informal care to address the increased needs of camp residents. In late August 1942, for instance, Toku's daughter Fumi and Toku's friend Masako came to see her. "I gave them a simple physical examination," she wrote. She also took care of her husband Yoshitomi, who shortly after their arrival at Minidoka "suddenly got stomach trouble.... He vomited and had diarrhea. I was busy the whole day taking care of him," she recorded in her diary. [26] In addition, she regularly visited friends who were sick in the camp hospital.

People looked out for each other. Friends and family cared for Toku when she became sick, even after she was hospitalized. In September 1942, only a month after arriving in Idaho, she had to be hospitalized. She suffered from several chronic ailments that were exacerbated by the stresses of wartime. She had hypertension and neuralgia, a condition in which pain radiates along the nerves. She often had difficulty sleeping because of headaches or pain in her hands and legs. [27]

To treat her ailments Toku combined western medicine with *kanpo*, traditional Japanese healing techniques, both before the war and in the camps. For example, she took drugs prescribed by doctors, such as her family physician Dr. Paul Suzuki, to reduce her high blood pressure. To relieve various aches and pains she received massages, sometimes from friends, but also from Dr. James M. Unosawa, an *Issei* osteopath and Dr. Fujii, "a massage specialist." [28] In addition, she received moxibustion treatments, a technique in which small cones of herbs are burned on the skin at specific points to promote healing. [29]

While she was hospitalized at Minidoka camp, she looked around and recognized sixteen of her friends in the nearby beds. Camp life was clearly taking its toll on the *Issei*. She also made observations about her caregivers, indicating that the nurses' aides were very kind. As for the trained nurses, "The sight of the nurses reminded me of past days when I was young and my heart was full," she revealed. [30] However, she was not left to the care of strangers. She had such a large community of friends and family that while in the hospital for one week she became worn out from so many visitors. [31]

24. Information on health care is located in the War Relocation Authority records in separate boxes and preserved in Record Group 210 – War Relocation Authority, National Archives, Washington, D.C.

25. Toku Shimomura's diary, 23 August and 4 September 1942; Sone, *Nisei Daughter*, 188-189, 192.

26. Toku Shimomura's diary, 24 August, 26 August, and 14 September 1942.

27. Toku Shimomura's diary, 13 February 1941, 10 April 1941, 1 May 1941, 23 August 1941, 26 April 1942, 21 October 1942.

28. Toku Shimomura's diary, 29 January 1941, 13 February 1941, 23 August 1941, 29 August 1941, 17 June 1942, 17 September 1942, 23 November 1942, 6 December 1942; Ito, Issei, 631-632.

29. Toku Shimomura's diary, January 2-5, 1941. On moxibustion see Ishihara Akira, "Kampō: Japan's Traditional Medicine," *Japan Quarterly*, v. 9 (1962): 429-37; Shigehisa Kuriyama, "Moxibustion," in *Encyclopedia of the History of Science, Technology, and Medicine in Non-Western Cultures*, ed. by Helaine Selin (Dordrecht, The Netherlands: Kluwer Academic Publishers, 1997), 748.

30. Toku Shimomura's diary, 18 September and 19 September 1942.

31. Toku Shimomura's diary, 20 September and 21 September 1942.

32. Toku Shimomura's diary, 23 September and 3 October 1942.

33. Toku Shimomura's diary, 14 May, 25 May, 26 May, 4 June, 12 June, 16 June, 27 June, 14 July, 30 July, 28 August, and 10 September 1942; Sone, *Nisei Daughter*, 195.

34. Toku Shimomura's diary, 21 October 1942.

35. Toku Shimomura's diary, 5 November, 6 November, 7 November, 10 November, 11 November, 14 November, and 16 December 1942.

36. Emily Abel, *Hearts of Wisdom: American Women Caring for Kin*, 1850-1940 (Cambridge: Harvard University Press, 2000), 1, 8, 172, 267, 269.

37. Toku Shimomura's diary, 20 November 1942, and see 29 September, 17 October, 20 October, and 23 October 1942.

Toku was ever the observant health care specialist. While she was hospitalized she noted in her diary that a case of food poisoning, likely caused by a can of blueberries, sent forty-five people to the hospital. Upon release from the hospital she also remarked that the state of sanitation in the camp was very poor, with flies swarming around the outhouse. Public health experts warned that flies carried germs and could contaminate food or water supplies. Apparently she had warned Dr. Suzuki, her family physician, that there would be problems. Not long after she expressed her concern there was an epidemic of diarrhea.[32]

Even though Toku engaged in caregiving work and a range of other activities, she often found camp life boring. Like other *Issei* women, Toku cleaned her family's room in the barracks, did laundry, took up knitting, visited with friends and family, took English classes, and went to choir practice, prayer meetings, and Bible classes.[33] Still, she grew tired of the monotony and was eager to find something more to do. In October 1942, after complaining that her blood pressure had gone sky high after she moved into camp, she remarked, "I'm starting to feel that I would like to work with sick people since I myself am in such bad condition."[34] Clearly, she had been attending to sick people all along. What she meant was that she wanted a job. Shortly after this she went to the job placement office and applied for one, and a month later she was offered a position. Sadly, Toku, who had spent over three decades working in the health care field, was told she could be a "checker" at the mess hall in the camp hospital. Her diary entries reveal nothing of the disappointment she might have felt. Instead, she took the job and wrote that it made her "feel like a worthy person again." However, after only four days the job placement office told her she could no longer work at the mess hall because the position had been promised to someone else. Undaunted, Toku later returned to the placement office to apply for another job. A month later she noted with disappointment that she had still not been offered any work.[35] As an older *Issei* woman, it appears that she was not wanted as a hired worker in the camp, even with her health care skills.

Despite camp restrictions on midwifery and Toku's own health problems, her role as a caregiver continued. She could not procure a paid job, but she still had her informal work. She labored to help others because people responded positively and it gave her genuine satisfaction. As scholars have shown, despite the burdens of giving care, it benefits not only the patients, but also the caregivers themselves.[36] Even a mere four days after Toku's release from the hospital, she had gone back to making house calls to others in their sickbeds, even at the hospital. She did not let up over the following months. She recorded in her diary when a friend was sick or had diarrhea, and when she gave someone a physical examination. At one point she made a call on Mrs. Hara who "was suffering from a dislocated leg."[37] Another time she wrote: "I made a call on Sister Sasaki's sickbed. I also visited Mrs. Kimura and Mrs. Tsugawa's sickbed." Health care work was a key aspect of what gave her life meaning.

In Seattle, Puyallup, and Minidoka, Toku Shimomura contributed to the well-being of Japanese Americans before and during the war. Although Toku and her husband Yoshitomi spent several years living in the assembly center and WRA camp, she was not isolated. Instead, throughout the evacuation and incarceration she lived with a strong sense of community. In 1944, she and her husband left Minidoka to go to Chicago where their son Kazuo (or Eddie) and his family, including grandson Roger, had already relocated. Finally, in 1945 the family moved back to Seattle where she rebuilt her network of friends and family in her former hometown. Toku was a comfort to people not only because she knew something about health care but also because she understood their hardships. In addition, she had developed intimate relationships with them and responded to them as individuals living through trying times. Such personal attention was especially valuable in the dehumanizing environment of the wartime camps. Her activities addressed not only physical needs, but also the emotional and spiritual dimensions of human beings.[38] Toku's diaries illustrate how she, like other *Issei* women, contributed to both community and personal survival through caregiving work.

38. Toku Shimomura's diary, 28 December 1942; Abel, *Hearts of Wisdom*, 4-5.

An Interview with Roger Shimomura, 15 June 2005

Keiki Reiko Hauseur

KH: In accordance with the title of this exhibition, *Minidoka Revisited*, I think it would be interesting to begin by revisiting the dominant interpretation of your well-known stylistic approach. Over the last twenty-six years you have received much recognition for your intriguing juxtaposing of subject matter from Japanese *ukiyo-e* woodblock prints and American popular culture as representative of your ethnic identity and the Japanese American experience. *Diary: December 7, 1941* (see catalog entry #4), is a great example. However, I think the images in your work function less as reflections of your ethnic identity and more as codified metaphors of your awareness of seeing and being seen. For example, your use of *ukiyo-e* images in your *Minidoka* and *Diary* series does not necessarily reflect your identification with, or understanding of, this artistic style, but rather your awareness of how the United States government viewed Japanese Americans as "enemy aliens." Could you please comment on how your usage of *ukiyo-e* imagery may function in your work as a metaphor for your awareness of how Japanese Americans are seen, dating back as early as your *Minidoka* series.

RS: Responding to the now well-known conversation at a Lawrence auction, the idea of introducing images from *ukiyo-e* woodblock prints was meant to provide future viewers a sarcastic, tongue-in-cheek response to the question of what was I? Of course I make paintings that look like that, because you think I look like that. For some reason, non-Asian Americans seemed to have difficulty distinguishing between the appearance of a Japanese American and a Japanese national. The presumption seems to have been that if one is of Asian descent, one must also be a foreigner.

I have to admit that when I decided to utilize the *ukiyo-e* style to tell the internment story in the *Minidoka* series, the use of narrative was new to me and I was wary of creating illustrations, rather than paintings. It didn't seem likely to me that anyone was going to buy paintings that chastised them for the internment debacle, so I felt like I would have to strategize some way for the work to end up in their living rooms. By making the work visually appealing, on an exotic-Asian level, I could then subtly impregnate the work with internment themes. I believed that at some point, the stench of the government blunder would inevitably rise to the surface of the work.

An interesting aside regarding the *Diary* series is that it was impossible to tell the camp story without actually depicting barbed wire. Since I knew of no friendly, sixteenth to eighteenth century Japanese equivalent of barbed wire, I was forced to faithfully represent it in seven of the paintings. I minimized its presence by using as little as a one-inch strand peeking out between two figures. Eventually all twenty-five paintings in the original *Diary* series sold, however the paintings that showed barbed wire were among the last to sell. Repeatedly, collectors bemoaned the presence of barbed wire in the paintings and, in fact, three offered to buy the work if the wire was painted out. I should add that the plan to maintain the decorative appearance of the work met with some controversy as some critics felt that in so doing, I was also perpetuating the stereotype that when Japanese Americans went to the privacy of their homes, they donned kimonos and ate with chopsticks.

Interestingly, almost twenty-five years later, I have returned to these notions about appearance again. Fully acknowledging the stigma of being forever foreign, I have just completed a new series of lithographs that depict *ukiyo-e* figures in internment campsites, not dissimilar to the *Minidoka* series. The intention this time is not to create a layer of ambiguity, but to directly address the implications of General DeWitt's proclamation that a "Jap's a Jap." A recent large painting entitled *Forever Foreigner* depicts myself as an *ukiyo-e* male figure amid a crowd of other similarly dressed figures styled in the woodblock manner. Similarly, the World War II stereotype, representing the ongoing threat of the Yellow Peril, was applied in both the *Stereotypes and Admonitions* series and the *Jap's a Jap* series.

KH: Your appropriation of *ukiyo-e* imagery and World War II stereotypical images reflect your awareness of how you, your grandmother (Toku), and Japanese Americans as a whole were viewed as Japanese by the United States government as well as an artistic strategy on your part. As the keynote speaker at the 2003 College Art Association conference you stated that your use of *ukiyo-e* images is ironic because they are just as exotic to you as to a person of non-Japanese decent. Could you please elaborate on this point?

RS: I found it ironic because I was just as intrigued by the Japanese people and culture as my white counterparts the first time I ever visited Japan in the early 1960s while doing military service. In the midst of that visit I came to realize how un-Japanese I actually was. Other than appearance, and a few Japanese customs that were processed through several generations of American culture, I realized that I was more entrenched in Euro-American culture. Yet, all my white G.I. buddies clustered around me constantly, because they thought I was going to show them how to navigate through Japan.

KH: This exhibition offers a unique opportunity to view three of your series (*Minidoka*, *Diary*, and *American Diary*) that deal solely with the Japanese American internment, specifically your grandmother's (Toku's) experience at Minidoka that she recorded in her diaries. I would like to discuss why you have revisited this historical event so many times and in so many ways. In looking at each series it is clear that your stylistic approach to each is very different; the Minidoka series is full of images appropriated from *ukiyo-e* masters, the *Diary* series presents a more obvious interweaving of Japanese and American subject matter, and the *American Diary* series displays an aesthetic that I would argue your own amalgamation of American and Japanese artistic styles. Could you please describe your thought process behind each series in regards to your decision of whether to incorporate or eliminate the presence of Japanese and American imagery within your work? Possibly elaborate on whether or not you mediate your selection of images depending on your anticipated audience and/or the intended message that you wish to convey.

RS: The process of art making has been a process of learning about my own identity. In other words the complexity of being an ethnic American was a process of understanding how I related to the world, and how that relationship changed as I learned more about that world. When art is seen as a by-product of a corresponding stage in life, it becomes understandable how revisiting one issue (internment) can be seen quite differently as one's perspective of life changes. The same can be said for stylistic approaches; they are subject to the same changes as one's relationship to the world develops.

In the *Minidoka* series, I previously explained the newness of narrative and the fear of illustration. The *Diary* series reflected the permission I had given myself to include contemporary objects that, despite their time incongruities, helped tell the story (diary entry), as well as provide the opportunity for some self-indulgence to paint the objects that I was collecting at the time.

American Diary was done mostly for educational purposes since that was the promise to the Civil Liberties Public Education Fund, which funded this series of work. I knew that a higher percentage of the audience would be Japanese American, young and old, many of them former internees. Since Japanese Americans were not my usual audience, I wanted to create a show that would appeal to them.

KH: It is evident that your process is not only interwoven with your personal growth and self-awareness but, also includes your consideration of who will be viewing the work. In addition to the earlier series discussed in this interview, this exhibition presents your latest series, *Stereotypes and Admonitions*, that encompasses various experiences you and other Asian Americans have encountered over roughly the span of your lifetime (sixty years). Instead of only using *ukiyo-e* subject matter as representative of Japanese Americans you chose stereotypical images from World War II of Japanese within American popular culture, such as in *Do You Speak English?* (see catalog entry #14). The derogatory images come mostly from comics and propaganda posters during this time. Could you please discuss why and how this choice came about? Also, how this contributes towards the message(s) conveyed by this series?

RS: The intention was that the *ukiyo-e* representations stood for the forever foreign notion discussed earlier. That presumption was, I believe, the cause of several of the incidents presented in paintings, such as *Florence, South Carolina* (see catalog entry #15). In this instance repeated explanations given by both myself and my wife (at the time), that we were both Americans born in the Pacific Northwest, were ignored. We finally came to realize that our assigned roles for that visit were that of Japanese tourists to this country. I guess we were more interesting to them that way.

The other representation was that of the World War II stereotype of the evil, sneaky, and inscrutable enemy. The specific depictions came directly from my collection of stereotypes, mostly acquired on Ebay auctions where Japanese people were seen as yellow-skinned, buck-toothed, slant-eyed monsters. The application in these cases were of myself as a reincarnation of the enemy, whether it be the Iranian during the hostage crises, *(Iranian Hostage Crises)*, or the pilot that attacked Pearl Harbor *(Remember Pearl Harbor)*.

KH: The stereotypical images allowed you to reference the injustices caused during World War II against American citizens and alert viewers of the danger of repeating the mistake of isolating an ethnic group and ignoring their civil rights due to fear. I think this exhibition is important because it highlights your latest series by presenting it almost in its entirety, yet maintains a relationship to your earlier works on Minidoka. *Not Pearl Harbor* (see catalog entry #23) and *Justified Internment* (see catalog entry #21) relate the Japanese American internment to the recent 9/11 attack on the United States. The *Stereotypes and Admonitions* series visually addresses the dangers of seeing Asian Americans as foreign Others, the physical and psychological violence that is caused, and the abuse of governmental power. You insert yourself through the stereo-typical World War II images to convey what if this was you. Could you please give a few thoughts on how important revisiting your personal experiences, your grandmother's diaries, and the experiences of other ethnic groups are to your work.

RS: My guess is that the personal experiences covered in *Stereotypes and Admonitions* had a collective impact upon my level of understanding of issues on sensitivity and tolerance. Certainly the incidents experienced after moving to Kansas, led directly into the first *Oriental Masterpiece* series. I doubt whether my work would have made that turn had it not been for the various experiences I had ranging from the internment memories as a small child, to attending inner city schools, living abroad, moving to the east coast, then to Kansas at a time when Asians were a rarity.

I seem to share my grandmother's belief that family history is important. I think she knew that as an immigrant, she was in a unique position in the history of this country. She recorded her story in a diary on a daily basis for fifty-six years, kept scrapbooks and photographs, and wrote journalistic accounts, *haiku* poetry and short stories. Revisiting my grandmother's diaries in my own work completed the circle that began with me giving her a new diary for Christmas every year, for the last fourteen years of her life.

While I do not consider myself a political activist outside of my work, I am a *Sansei* who learned the lessons taught by the Black Power movement of the 60s. I have watched the various ethnic communities step up when their turn came, and make tremendous headway towards achieving equal respect: however, even after all of the seeming gains, the series of events that followed 9/11 was a confirmation that this government is capable of repeating the mistakes of World War II, and that racism in this country, is still alive and well at the highest levels of our government.

KH: Yes, this exhibition demonstrates how important it is to remember, discuss, teach, and learn from the Japanese American internment; the mistake of isolating and labeling ethnic groups as different to justify inhumane acts. While respecting your Japanese heritage as well as your American cultural roots, I see your appropriation of *ukiyo-e* imagery as ironic because many people see your work as reflecting an inherent Japanese knowledge and categorize you as a Japanese artist, like that expressed in your painting *History of Art* (see catalog entry #18). It is like a double-edged sword, you want people to be aware and respectful of difference as part of America and it's culture, but, also, this recognition of your ethnic identity can overshadow your actual identification with American art. Could you please give some thoughts on how you tackle this matter in your work?

RS: It's beyond my control. If my identification with American art were of paramount importance, I wouldn't venture down the path that I do. While the pill is bitter sometimes, it comes with the territory. It, once again, underscores the fact that Asian people in this country are usually recognized first as foreigners, not Americans. I hear many mainstream critics say that so-called marginalized artists only ghettoize themselves by emphasizing their differences, but would those same critics tell people that live in neighborhood ghettos, to simply move out to solve the problem? The kind of art that we do is not based in style, like Impressionism or Abstract Expressionism, but it is fundamental to some of the basic reasons why art was made in the first place: to reflect upon oneself and their position in their society.

KH: Your work provides a door that opens discussion and awareness of American history, society, and art. Each painting in this exhibition is accompanied by a textual description that describes the work. Could you discuss the importance of the text as a piece of the complete artwork?

RS: In this series I believed that in order for any interaction to begin, both text and image should be objectively provided to the viewer. After that, I felt that each person would respond differently, most likely responding more to one or the other. Personally, I hoped that the audience might engage the issues at hand rather than be wowed by the visual statement. Also, I had hoped that the work would continue its life as the topics would continue to be debated long after leaving the gallery.

KH: Mr. Shimomura, you have stated previously that during the selling of *Diary* series only nine of the twenty-five paintings sold, requested the textual description with the work. Have you encountered the same results with your *Stereotypes and Admonitions* series?

RS: Collectors were clearly interested, this time, in having a copy of the incident that sparked the painting. Twenty-five years have passed since doing the initial *Diary* series, and I think this change is primarily due to the fact that people have become a little more sophisticated about the role that art plays in our society.

KH: It is reassuring that this positive change has created opportunities to reexamine art through another lens. You continue to search for ways to address, visualize, and vocalize problems of racism using various mediums: painting, sculpture, performance, and installation. What do you anticipate as your next project?

RS: A couple of years ago I made a small foray into critiquing Japan over the Rape of Nanking massacre. I made two large paintings, but no one seemed to connect with either the paintings or with the gravity of the topic. Upon recently seeing the exhibition *Little Boy: The Arts of Japan's Exploding Subculture* in New York, I once again feel compelled to return to the subject of Japan's refusal to take responsibility for its complicity in not only the Rape of Nanking, but for other dark moments in their violent past. How a country with such profound issues can also be represented by the culture of *kawai* (cute) intrigues and disturbs me so much so that I'm thinking about addressing this in my next series of paintings.

KH: Thank you for your time. I look forward to your future exhibitions.

Minidoka Revisited | Catalog of Paintings

Minidoka No. 3 (Diary)

1

1978
Acrylic on Canvas, 60" x 72"
Spencer Museum of Art, University of Kansas

Minidoka No. 4 (Dream)

2

1978
Acrylic on Canvas, 60" x 72"
Collection of Fred Magenheimer

Minidoka No. 6 (No-No Boy)

3

1979
Acrylic on Canvas, 60" x 72"
Collection of Bea Kiyohara

Diary: Dec. 7, 1941 (Version #3)

4

c. 1983
Acrylic on Canvas, 60" x 50"
Collection of Burdett and Michel Loomis

DIARY ENTRY: *When I came back from church I heard the dreamlike news that Japanese airplanes had bombed Hawaii. I was surprised beyond belief. I sat in front of the radio and listened to the news all day. It was said that this morning at 6 a.m. Japan declared war on the United States. Our future has become gloomy. I pray that God will stay with us.*

Diary: Aug. 27, 1942

5

c. 1983
Acrylic on Canvas, 50" x 60"
Collection of Michael and Karen Herman

DIARY ENTRY: *Storm. What a view! I have never seen such a dust storm.
I stayed in my room and looked out the window. It was so dark we were
afraid to move.*

*Pessimistic words came out of everyone's mouth.
We were sent to such a harsh place.*

American Diary: April 21, 1942 (Seattle)

6

1997
Acrylic on Canvas, 11" x 14"
Collection of Esther Weissman

DIARY ENTRY: *At last the order for evacuation was given formally by General DeWitt. There were some limitations to the first move. Kazuo (son) along with some others will leave here on the 28th as an advance party. In haste we prepared for the leave.*

American Diary: May 16, 1942 (Camp Harmony)

7

1997
Acrylic on Canvas, 11" x 14"
Collection of Dr. and Mrs. Lawrence Y. Matsuda

DIARY ENTRY: *Fine weather today, although it showered in the evening. In the afternoon Kazuo carried Roger in. I was able to enjoy him for only a few minutes. Today the process of accommodating the 8,000 Japanese from the Seattle area finished. The camp became very lively.*

Jap's a Jap #6

8

2000
Acrylic on Canvas, 36" x 48"
Collection of Roger Shimomura

9

How to Tell the Difference
Between the Japanese and the Chinese
(Yellow Rat Bastard)

2000
Mixed Media, Acrylic on Canvas and Objects, 72" x 96" x 9"
Collection of Roger Shimomura

Mr. Wong's Theatre Company

2001
Acrylic on Canvas, 60" x 72"
Bernice Steinbaum Gallery

10

Stereotypes and Admonitions: Abercrombie & Fitch

11

2003
Acrylic on Canvas, 20" x 24"
Collection of Dr. and Mrs. Corey Casper

NARRATIVE: *In April 2002, retail clothing store Abercrombie & Fitch introduced a new line of T-shirts depicting smiling men with slanted eyes wearing conical hats. The T-shirts carried slogans such as "Buddha Bash" and "Wok-n-Bowl." Asian American groups responded quickly, complaining that these images and phrases were blatant examples of racial stereotyping. Protests began at Abercrombie & Fitch stores nationwide.*

After instructing all stores to remove the T-shirts, a spokesman for Abercrombie & Fitch said the company felt the shirts would be especially loved by the Asian American community and would be seen as cheeky, irreverent and funny. He said he was surprised by the hostile reception the merchandise received.

12

Stereotypes and Admonitions:
Back to the West Coast

2003
Acrylic on Canvas, 20" x 24"
Greg Kucera Gallery

NARRATIVE: *While coordinator of the Freshman Foundation Program at the University of Kansas in the fall of 1972, Roger called a meeting of the teaching assistants in the Basic Design Program. He invited one of the professors in the Design Department to talk about what he expected his future majors to learn in the Foundation Program. Roger invited this particular professor because he had been quite vocal at faculty meetings regarding his dissatisfaction with the way basic design was currently being taught.*

When Roger expressed his reasons for supporting the existing design curriculum, the professor lashed out by saying, "This here is proof that students at Kansas should be taught by faculty that are from this region. Shimomura's ideas should be practiced on the West Coast where other Oriental people like him live."

Stereotypes and Admonitions:
Denny's Incident

13

2003
Acrylic on Canvas, 20" x 24"
Greg Kucera Gallery

NARRATIVE: *In the fall of 1997, several Asian and Asian American students waited to be seated at a Denny's Restaurant in Syracuse, New York. After waiting inside for some time without any acknowledgement, the group placed their names on the waiting list. Groups of white males, who arrived subsequently, experienced no delay and were seated immediately. When the students questioned why they were not being seated, they were asked to leave the restaurant and were escorted outside by two Denny's security guards.*

Once outside, one of the guards pushed a Japanese student. Suddenly, a group of at least ten white males came out of the restaurant shouting racial epithets and attacking a few of the students. As the victims' friends came to their aid, they were also attacked. The Denny's security guards stood by and watched, but did not step in to help. Finally, two African American students, who had also been waiting inside, broke in and pulled away the white males. By then, four of the Asian American students were injured, two beaten unconscious. When the police finally arrived, the fight had ended and the group of white males had left the scene.

Five months later, following an investigation, the Onondaga County District Attorney's office concluded that no hate crime had been committed. The District Attorney claimed that everything, from beginning to end, appeared to have been orchestrated by the Asian American students to further their political cause.

Stereotypes and Admonitions: Do You Speak English?

2003
Acrylic on Canvas, 20" x 24"
Collection of Jon and Mary Shirley

NARRATIVE: *During the summer of 2001, a group of Asian American youth, on a field trip to an art studio in downtown Seattle, were using a marked crosswalk that had no pedestrian signal. A Seattle police officer began yelling at them from the patrol car, "Don't you know how to cross the street? Do you speak English?" Caucasian pedestrians were crossing in the same manner without receiving any reprimand from the police. Evan after the students were lined up against the wall and spoke English to the police, the officer kept asking, "Do you speak English? Are you foreigners?" The students were all verbally harassed as the officers patted them down.*

Soon thereafter, three additional police cars arrived on the scene. In anger, one of the officers yelled to one of the members of the group who was attempting to mediate, "I've been to your country before — when I was in the Army!"

15

Stereotypes and Admonitions: Florence, South Carolina

2003
Acrylic on Canvas, 20″ x 24″
Collection of Anton and Marie Ursini

NARRATIVE: *In 1969, after graduating from Syracuse University, Roger and his first wife visited their good friend Alvin, in Florence, South Carolina. Alvin's mother threw a dinner party for her friends and relatives, all long-time residents of Florence. The purpose of the party was for everyone to meet Alvin's "friends from Japan" despite Roger and his wife's repeated insistence that they were Americans who happened to be of Japanese descent.*

During pre-dinner cocktails, Roger was introduced to Fran, one of Alvin's favorite aunts. Fran was a school teacher and college graduate, often referred to as the "intellectual" of the family. As introductory pleasantries were exchanged, Fran asked Roger his name. Roger said his first name and then, in very crisp English, Fran repeated her question to Roger. After Roger repeated his first name, Fran commented very slowly, so as not to be misunderstood, "Well, I guess my name sounds as weird to you as yours does to me."

Stereotypes and Admonitions: Fox and Banzai

16

2003
Acrylic on Canvas, 20" x 24"
Greg Kucera Gallery

NARRATIVE: *In 2003, FOX network introduced "Banzai," a British game show spoof that featured a heavily accented Japanese narrator, Caucasian actresses in geisha costumes, and actors who would strike exaggerated martial arts poses. A spokesman for the Japanese American Citizen's League claimed that the program caricatured Japanese in the worst possible way through buffoonery and tasteless stereotyping.*

Scott Grogin, Vice President of Corporate Communications for FOX, reported that the show received high ratings from a targeted test audience of young male viewers. He justified it saying, "We feel that Banzai is a very funny, edgy game show, an equal opportunity offender, simply a parody, fun and not offensive."

Stereotypes and Admonitions:
The Gook

2003
Acrylic on Canvas, 20" x 24"
Hallie Ford Museum of Art

NARRATIVE: *One Saturday afternoon in the summer of 1976, Roger visited Seattle's tourist-filled Pike Place Market. While walking along the crowded stalls, Roger noticed that walking in front of him was a tattooed Caucasian male with long hair, wearing a leather headband, cutoff jeans and no shirt. The man appeared to be in a highly agitated state and was walking in an exaggerated fashion while swearing profusely.*

As Roger began to pass him, the man yelled at Roger, "Hey Gook, I killed your fuckin' brother in 'Nam. I killed your mother and father, too!" Then for at least thirty more feet the man walked beside Roger, screaming about having "killed hundreds of VCs and Chinks just like you!"

18

Stereotypes and Admonitions:
The History of Art

2003
Acrylic on Canvas, 20" x 24"
Collection of Marilyn Domoto Webb

NARRATIVE: *Several years ago, Roger had a conversation with an art history colleague who was writing a textbook on the history of art. She informed Roger that she had included his name and painting with other American artists in the chapter on contemporary American art. She also said she could not promise his name would survive the editing process due to a difference of opinion with her editor, who felt Roger would be best defined as a contemporary Japanese painter rather than a contemporary American painter.*

19

20 Stereotypes and Admonitions: Housing Discrimination

2003
Acrylic on Canvas, 20" x 24"
Greg Kucera Gallery

NARRATIVE: *A study released July 1, 2003, by the Department of Housing and Urban Development shows that among Asians and Pacific Islanders attempting to buy or rent a home, one out of every five experience some discrimination — a rate similar to that of African Americans and Hispanics. The study was conducted in Anaheim/Santa Ana, Chicago, Honolulu, Los Angeles, Minneapolis, New York, Oakland, San Diego, San Francisco, San Jose, and Washington, D.C.*

This is the first time HUD has measured the extent of housing discrimination against Asians and Pacific Islanders.

Stereotypes and Admonitions:
Iran Hostage Crisis

2003
Acrylic on Canvas, 20" x 24"
Collection of Catherine Hillenbrand

NARRATIVE: *During the Iran Hostage Crisis of 1987, Roger was jogging on a country road approximately a mile from his house when a pickup truck carrying two men approached. When the truck got within 50 feet, it suddenly veered toward him causing Roger to jump into a gully beside the road. As Roger leapt from the road the driver leaned out the window and flipped Roger his middle finger, yelling as he sped off, "That's for your ayatollah, you Chinaman!"*

Stereotypes and Admonitions:
Justified Internment

21

2003
Acrylic on Canvas, 20" x 24"
Greg Kucera Gallery

NARRATIVE: *On February 4, 2003, U.S. Representative Howard Coble, Chairman of the Judiciary Subcommittee on Crime, Terrorism and Homeland Security, participated in a radio call-in program about national security. When a caller suggested Arabs in the United States should be confined, Coble disagreed. However, Coble did say he agreed with President Franklin D. Roosevelt who established the internment camps for Japanese Americans during World War II.*

Following a furor raised by the Asian community and others, the Republican Representative from North Carolina attempted to clarify his remarks by saying that the internment camps were as much for the Japanese Americans' own safety as for national security.

22

Stereotypes and Admonitions:
Not an Indian, (Variation #2)

2003
Acrylic on Canvas, 20" x 24"
Greg Kucera Gallery

NARRATIVE: *In the spring of 1970, after moving to Lawrence, Kansas, Roger went to Wilson's Department store to buy his wife a coat for her birthday. Wilson's would not take Visa or MasterCard at the time and required that charges be made to a Wilson's credit card only. The salesperson told Roger that he could fill out an application and obtain immediate approval to charge the coat.*

As directed, Roger went to the second floor credit counter and requested an application. The woman behind the counter said it was against Wilson's policy to issue credit cards to Indians. When Roger said he was not an Indian, the woman told him she did not believe him. Roger then asked to speak to the manager.

When the manager arrived, the woman behind the counter told him she had dutifully informed Roger that it was store policy not to grant credit cards to Indians. The manager examined Roger carefully and then said, "She's right, sir. We don't give credit cards to Indians." Roger repeated to the manager that he was not an Indian, whereupon the manager said, "You got any proof that you ain't, mister?"

23

Stereotypes and Admonitions:
Not Pearl Harbor

2003
Acrylic on Canvas, 20" x 24"
Collection of Driek and Michael Zirinsky

NARRATIVE: *Since the horrible tragedy of September II, 2001, numerous comparisons have been made to the 1941 attack on Pearl Harbor. For many reasons this comparison has made millions of Japanese Americans anxious — reminding them of the injustice of their wrongful internment during WWII. Today, many members of the Islamic religion, Arab Americans, Middle Eastern Americans, and anyone who looks like "them," encounter similar intimidation, violence, and racial profiling.*

This painting depicts the faces of WWII Japanese enemy stereotypes, now bearded and turbaned as the stereotypical terrorists. In the background, in place of the 9/11 planes on their kamikaze-style mission, Japanese Zero planes head toward their targets.

Stereotypes and Admonitions:
Passé

24

2003
Acrylic on Canvas, 20" x 24"
Greg Kucera Gallery

NARRATIVE: *In 2002, Roger was asked to submit a proposal for a percent for arts project on a university campus in the state of Washington. The submitted drawing proposed a mural which would explore the complex question of whether America would be better off continuing to be thought of as a "melting pot," or whether it might be more relevant today for America to be more like a "tossed salad." A month later Roger was told that he was not awarded the commission due in part to an art historian on the panel who said that the subject was "soooo passé."*

Artist's Biography

ROGER SHIMOMURA'S paintings, prints and theatre pieces address socio-political issues of Asian America and have often been inspired by 56 years of diaries kept by his late immigrant grandmother.

He received his undergraduate degree from the University of Washington in Seattle and his graduate degree from Syracuse University, New York. He has had over 100 solo exhibitions of his paintings and prints, and has presented his experimental theater pieces at such venues as the Franklin Furnace, New York City, Walker Art Center, Minneapolis and The Smithsonian Institution. He is the recipient of four National Endowment for the Arts Fellowships in painting and performance art, a McKnight Fellowship, the Kansas Governor's Artist Award, a Civil Liberties Public Education Fund Fellowship, the Joan Mitchell Foundation Award, and was the first artist internationally to be awarded a Japan Foundation Grant, as well as the first in the state to receive the Kansas Arts Commission Artist Fellowship in Painting. In the fall of 1990, he was appointed the Dayton Hudson Distinguished Visiting Professor at Carleton College, Northfield, Minnesota. Professor Shimomura has been a visiting artist and lectured on his work at almost 200 universities and art museums across the country. In 1999, the Seattle Urban League designated a scholarship under his name that since has been awarded annually to a Seattle resident pursuing a career in art. Recently, the College Art Association presented him with the Artist Award for Most Distinguished Body of Work for 2001, for his 4-year, 12-museum national tour of the painting exhibition, *An American Diary*. In February 2003 he delivered the keynote address at the 91st meeting of that association in New York City.

At the University of Kansas where he taught since 1969 he was designated a University Distinguished Professor in 1994, the first so honored in the history of the School of Fine Arts on that campus. He has been awarded 20 general research grants from his university, and in 1998, was the recipient of the Higuchi Research Award, the highest annual honor bestowed upon a faculty member in the Humanities and Social Sciences. In the fall of 2002, he received the Chancellor's Club Career Teaching Award for sustained excellence in teaching and dedication to students at the University of Kansas. In 2004 he retired from teaching and started the Shimomura Faculty Research Support Fund, an endowment to support faculty research in the Department of Art.

Shimomura's personal papers are being collected by the Archives of American Art, Smithsonian Institution in Washington, D.C. He is represented by The Flomenhaft Gallery, New York City, Greg Kucera Gallery, Seattle, Bernice Steinbaum Gallery, Miami, and Jan Weiner Gallery, Kansas City.

About the Essayists

ROGER DANIELS is Charles Phelps Taft Professor Emeritus of History at the University of Cincinnati. He served as consultant to the Presidential Commission on Wartime Relocation and Internment of Civilians and is a planning committee member for the immigration museum on Ellis Island. His many recent works include *Prisoners Without Trial: Japanese Americans in World War II* (2nd. Ed., 2004); *Guarding the Golden Door: American Immigration Policy and Immigrants since 1882* (2004), *Not Like Us: Immigration and Minorities in America, 1890-1924* (1997); and an expanded edition of *Coming to America: A History of Immigration Policy and Immigration* (2002).

KRYSTAL REIKO HAUSEUR recently received her M.A. in Art History, specializing in Asian American art, from San Francisco State University and will be continuing her doctoral studies at the University of California, Irvine. Her M.A. thesis focused on the art of Roger Shimomura. She began researching Asian American artists during her undergraduate studies at U.C.L.A. and has since been awarded a summer research fellowship by the Smithsonian Institution and interned as a curatorial assistant at the Fine Arts Museum, (DeYoung), San Francisco for an upcoming national exhibition.

WILLIAM W LEW is a Professor in the Department of Art of Clemson University where he teaches art history. His research interest in past years has focused on the artistic accomplishments of Asian Americans. He has followed the artistic development of the Japanese American painter Roger Shimomura since the early 1970s. Lew's research on this artist includes the following articles: "Journey to Minidoka: The Paintings of Roger Shimomura," and "Roger Shimomura: Return of the Yellow Peril." Professor Lew is the principle investigator in this project.

126

ERIC L. MULLER is the George R. Ward Professor of Law at the University of North Carolina, Chapel Hill. His areas of expertise include criminal justice and constitutional issues. The eviction and detention of persons of Japanese ancestry in the U.S. during World War II have served as a touchstone for many of his publications, including the book, *Free to Die for Their Country: The Story of the Japanese American Draft Resisters in World War II*, and the articles: "Constitutional Conscience," "12/7 and 9/11: War, Liberties and the Lessons of History," "A Penny for their Thoughts? Draft Resistance at the Poston Relocation Center," "Apologies or Apologists? Remembering the Japanese American Internment in Wyoming," and "Inference or Impact? Racial Profiling and The Internment's True Legacy."

SUSAN L. SMITH is a Professor in the Department of History and Classics at the University of Alberta in Edmonton, Alberta, Canada. Her areas of expertise and research interests include the USA, women, medicine, and race/ethnicity. Her research in Asian American studies includes a recently published book entitled *Japanese American Midwives: Culture, Community, and Health Politics, 1880-1950* (University of Illinois Press, 2005), and a number of articles, including: "Medicine, Midwifery, and the State: Japanese Americans and Health Care in Hawai'i, 1885-1945," and "Women Health Workers and the Color Line in the Japanese American 'Relocation Centers' of World War II." One of the foci of her research on Japanese American midwives was Toku Shimomura, the artist's grandmother (and the source of inspiration for the artist's Diary and American Diary series).

DANIEL WUESTE is an Associate Professor of Philosophy and Director of the Robert J. Rutland Center for Ethics at Clemson University. His research and writing focus on issues in three areas: legal philosophy, social and political philosophy, and professional ethics; he is particularly interested in what ethicists can learn from legal philosophy and vice versa. His research has appeared in various journals, including *Cornell Law Review, Harvard Journal of Law and Public Policy,* and the *Canadian Journal of Law and Jurisprudence*. He is the author of the chapter on professional ethics in *The Biomedical Engineering Handbook*, and the editor of *Professional Ethics and Social Responsibility*. His article "The Realist's Challenge in Professional Ethics: Taking Some Cues from Legal Philosophy" recently appeared in *Professional Ethics.*